TROYTE GRIFFITH

TROYTE GRIFFITH
Malvern Architect and Elgar's Friend

Jeremy M. Hardie

Foreword
Michael Peach, RIBA

Troyte Griffith: Malvern Architect and Elgar's Friend
Jeremy M. Hardie

Published by Aspect Design 2012
Malvern, Worcestershire, United Kingdom.
Reprinted with corrections August 2012.

Designed and Printed by Aspect Design
89 Newtown Road, Malvern, Worcs. WR14 1PD
United Kingdom
Tel: 01684 561567
E-mail: allan@aspect-design.net
Website: www.aspect-design.net

Cover Design Copyright © 2012 Aspect Design
Original image of Malvern Priory Gateway from the Malvern Library collection.
Title page shows the drawing of Arthur Troyte Griffith by Victor Hume Moody
from the Catherine Moody collection.

ISBN 978-1-908832-10-8

*Dedicated to the memory of
the late Catherine Moody.*

CONTENTS

LIST OF ILLUSTRATIONS

ACKNOWLEDGEMENTS

I am extremely grateful to the many individuals and organisations that have helped in the preparation of this book.

Firstly, my thanks are due to the executors of the estate of the late Catherine Moody who kindly allowed me to retain and use the various papers and notes about Troyte Griffith that she had assembled over many years.

Michael Peach was involved with researching Troyte Griffith's buildings in the 1970s, together with Catherine Moody and other members of the Malvern Architectural Society. In addition to writing the foreword to this book, Michael has generously shared with me his photographs of some of the buildings, read through most of my early drafts, and provided welcome encouragement.

Martin Bird, editor of the *Elgar Society Journal,* has very kindly made available his transcripts of correspondence between Troyte Griffith and Edward Elgar, as well as selected entries from the Elgar diaries. He has also been a most useful source of relevant background information.

The Elgar Birthplace Museum has been an invaluable source of material, including illustrations and documents. I am most grateful to Cathy Sloan and Sue Fairchild for all their help in finding this material and for arranging permission to quote from correspondence between Troyte Griffith and the Elgar family, including letters for which the transcripts are numbered 7269, 7380, 7332, 7352, 7369, 7357, 7246, 7362, 7351, 7318, 7319, 7243, 7363, 4980, 7297, 7268, 7284, 7231, 387, 493, 7382, 7372, 7393, 628, 266, 7304, 7303, 887, and 7371.

Numerous other libraries, museums and archives have been consulted, and my thanks go particularly to Catherine Lees and staff of the Malvern Library, Worcestershire County Museum (Anita Blythe, Collections Officer), Worcestershire Records Office, Harrow School (Rita Boswell, Archivist), Haileybury School (Toby Parker, Archivist), Shrewsbury School (Mike Morrogh, Archivist), Harrow Libraries, Bristol Drama Department (Heather Romaine, Keeper of Theatre Archives), British Library, Malvern Museum (Brian Iles, Curator), British Association (Rupa Kundu, Personal Assistant to Chief Executive), LSE Library (Sue Donnelly, Archivist), Greater Manchester County Record Office (Kevin Bolton, Archives), RIBA Library (Peter Kent and staff), Birmingham University Library (Philippa Bassett, Senior Archivist), Malvern Priory (Alistair Sawes, Archivist), and Malvern Chess Club (Brian Turner, Secretary).

For permission to use particular illustrations and quotations I am most grateful to the editor of the *Malvern Gazette*,* the editor of the *Musical Times* (Antony Bye), the editor of *Worcestershire Life* (Jane Sullivan), Lebrecht Music and Arts (Stella Calvert-Smith), Malvern Library (Catherine Lees), Jerrold Northrop Moore, Elgar's distinguished biographer, who has shared valuable information with me and kindly allowed me to include his photograph of Lilian Griffith, Mrs Renée Morris Young, Arthur Reynolds and John Norris.

My thanks also go to the Malvern Concert Club (Joseph Brand, Chairman and Linda Jennings, Secretary) for permission to use illustrative material from the club's archives, and to the archivist, Michael Messenger, for providing much useful information.

I have had extensive discussions and correspondence with many other people who have been most helpful and encouraging during the preparation of this book, including Kevin Allen, Peter Bradford, Denis Chetwood, Glynis Dray, Philip Duckworth, Roger Hall-Jones, John Harcup, Wilfred Harper, David Howe, Michael Kennedy, Elizabeth Kerr, John Oates, David Prentice, Arthur Reynolds, Jane Ratcliffe, Andrew Probert, Peter Smith, Peter

---

* All material attributed to the *Malvern Gazette* is courtesy and copyright of the *Malvern Gazette*.

Sutton, Roger Sutton and other members of the Malvern Civic Society, Michael Trott, and Mrs Renée Morris Young. Several of these individuals have kindly made available their own notes about Troyte Griffith, or copies of pictures. I am also very grateful to Charles Morgan for allowing me to quote from his address at Catherine Moody's funeral.

I have had extremely useful contacts with Troyte Griffith's great- niece, Mrs Penny Dodds, to whom I am most indebted for permission to quote from some of Troyte's writings and for the reproduction of the portraits of George and Harriet Griffith.

For the picture of Troyte's altar frontal for St Andrew's Church, Pau, and for much background material, my sincere thanks go to Thea Downie, Liz Rushton and Father Ian Naylor. Thanks are also due to Canon Ian Woodward of St John the Baptist Church, Bere Regis, for the picture of the reredos in that church.

In order to visit and photograph many of Troyte's buildings, I have received generous assistance from a number of house owners, including Mr and Mrs C. Moir, Mr and Mrs D. Blundell, Mr and Mrs P. Westbury, Mr and Mrs A. Cowpe, Mr and Mrs J. Daniels, Mr and Mrs J. Price, Mr and Mrs N. Goodwin, Mr and Mrs H. Vivian, Annabel Pilfold and Diana Morgan, Mr and Mrs M. Dunwoody, Mr and Mrs S. Canning, Mr and Mrs J. Roskams and Mrs A. Lohoar.

Two local estate agents in Great Malvern, John Goodwin, and Allan, Morris and Ashton, helpfully allowed me to look round and photograph vacant Troyte Griffith houses that were on the market during the preparation of this book.

Philip Moere, principal, showed me around Abbey College, and, right at the start of this project, Clifford Prosser very kindly gave me a conducted tour of All Saints Church, Lower Wyche.

Every effort has been made to establish who owns the copyright for material used in this book and to seek appropriate permission for its inclusion. However, sincere apologies to anyone I may inadvertently have failed to acknowledge.

I am very grateful to my good friend Eric Midwinter for his most helpful and constructive comments on the manuscript and for all his encouragement, and to Dan Smith and his colleagues at Aspect Design.

Finally, thanks to my wife, Margaret, for her unfailing support and for putting up with me being so absorbed in the preparation of this book, to the exclusion of many other things I might usefully have been doing for the last two to three years.

FOREWORD

A friend once described Troyte Griffith to me as 'Something for Malvern' and this book shows the truth of this statement. Troyte, in a quiet, modest way, made a significant contribution to the building landscape and the musical and artistic culture of Malvern and, of course, through his friendship with Elgar who for several years lived in and around Malvern.

My own interest lies in Troyte's visible work as an architect from 1896 until his death in 1942. He would have known the rewards and sometimes difficulties of running a small practice in Malvern. He wanted to retain his individuality and was somewhat reluctant to join organisations where there were people who might have advanced his career. It was Catherine Moody, one time head of the School of Art in Malvern and founder of the Malvern Architectural Society who encouraged me to study Troyte's buildings. We worked together on a presentation about his buildings for a Malvern festival event and it was always her wish that one day more recognition would be given to his buildings, his art and the part he played in Malvern life. When Jeremy Hardie moved into one of Troyte's houses near to Catherine she inspired him to take an interest in architecture and to write this comprehensive book about the man, his friends, and the connection with architecture, art and music. It is good that Professor Hardie has been able to speak to some of the present owners of these houses that Troyte built. I feel that, unlike other, perhaps better known architects, Troyte was not overly possessive about houses he built. He wanted them to be typical of their period, adaptable and fitting in with their sites around the hills and above all a comfortable home to live in.

Malvern Concert Club is still a thriving force within Malvern today but the influence that Troyte had on its inauguration and early days is probably not fully appreciated. The strength of this book is in bringing together strands of information which have been available but have been scattered. For instance, there were details of Troyte's buildings and examples of his art mentioned and illustrated in several articles and publications but they have never been brought together. Again, Troyte has often been mentioned as a friend of Elgar's, mainly because of the inclusion of him as one of 'my friends within' in the *Enigma Variations,* but the close family friendship has not previously been so fully explored.

Catherine would have been delighted to know that her long term ambition of publishing a work about Troyte has been fulfilled in such a competent manner. I am sure she would be even more delighted if a gallery could be established in Malvern to show the work of Troyte and perhaps some of her own and her father's work and also that of other contemporary artists who are making their homes in Malvern.

Michael Peach
Architect

CATHERINE MOODY:
A DEDICATION

I first became interested in Arthur Troyte Griffith (Troyte) and his work at the beginning of 2007 when my wife and I purchased Delve End, one of a group of three houses in Malvern that he had designed near the junction of Cockshot Road and Albert Road North. Whilst trying to find out more about the architect from sources in the local library and elsewhere, it soon became apparent that much of the available material originated from Catherine Moody, the local artist, author and historian, who had written and spoken extensively about Troyte. On further investigation, quite fortuitously, I discovered that Catherine lived just round the corner from us at Lorne Lodge in Sling Lane and I was soon able to establish contact with her. This led to many meetings, telephone conversations and exchanges of information over the next two and a half years until, sadly, she died in December, 2009 at the age of eighty-nine.

I quickly realised that Catherine, although confined to the house and suffering from failing eyesight, was as sharp as ever intellectually and that she had strongly held opinions on many subjects. Every conversation with her was rather like a history lesson for me and I was always stimulated by the depth and scope of her knowledge about art, crafts, architecture, literature, music, local history and many other topics. She was also full of fascinating recollections and anecdotes about the many interesting people she had met and conversed or corresponded with during her life.

Catherine's father, Victor Hume Moody (1896–1990), was a distinguished artist who painted in the style known as Modern Realism and became head of the Malvern School of Art in 1935, in succession to Illingworth Varley. Victor Moody knew Troyte Griffith personally and many other distinguished people in the arts world, including George Bernard Shaw, whose portrait he painted on more than one occasion. Catherine eventually succeeded her father as head of the School of Art on his retirement in 1962. She also became chairman of the Malvern Architectural Society which, in 1978, put on a series of exhibitions and lectures about Troyte as part of the Malvern Fringe Festival.

Lorne Lodge, Catherine Moody's house in Sling Lane, Malvern.

Catherine Olive Moody was born in 1920 and educated at the Royal College of Art, from where she qualified as an art teacher. She worked at Manchester School of Art before joining her father on the staff of the Malvern School of Art. As well as being a distinguished artist and teacher, Catherine took a great interest in the geology, wild life, history, industry and many other aspects of the life of Malvern and the surrounding countryside. She wrote a book about the architecture of the area entitled *Silhouette of Malvern*, published in 1953, and produced an invaluable audio-tape about Troyte Griffith in 1998.

Front cover of Catherine Moody's
audio-tape about Troyte Griffith.

Front cover of Catherine Moody's
book *Silhouette of Malvern*.

At Her funeral in Malvern Priory on 18 December, 2009, attended by many of her friends and former pupils, the main tribute was given by Charles Morgan.

Some of Charles's thoughts about Catherine were also quoted in the obituary which was published in the *Malvern Gazette* on 9 October, 2009:

> Throughout her life she was an inspiration to many people who lived in the Malvern Hills area, combining her encyclopaedic knowledge of art and local history with a remarkable vision for a better future.
>
> Catherine will be missed by all her friends. She held group meetings for people who wanted to make a difference right up to the end of her life. It was impossible to leave her presence without feeling the need to Google the names of a multitude of people that she had mentioned in discussion. Her vision saw no conflict between the best of art and science. One only

Front and back pages of the Order of Service for Catherine Moody's funeral.

Catherine Moody in her studio at Lorne Lodge in 2007.

hopes that there will be people like her in the future to carry on improving our world and the objects in it.

Catherine generously shared with me her unique and extensive collection of papers and other material concerning Troyte Griffith and I am most grateful that the executors of her estate have very kindly allowed me to continue to use these documents. It had been our intention to write something together but, sadly, we were not able to complete this task before her untimely death. I am therefore pleased to dedicate this book to the memory of Catherine Moody, a truly remarkable woman. I hope she would approve.

The picture of Catherine was taken for an article about her which appeared in *Worcestershire Life* magazine in December, 2007 (photograph courtesy of Ian Cameron, *Worcestershire Life*).

INTRODUCTION

Anyone who has listened to Elgar's *Enigma Variations* will no doubt be familiar with the fast, boisterous and rather jerky rhythms of 'Variation' VII, which is named 'Troyte' after the subject of this book, the architect Arthur Troyte Griffith. As mentioned in the dedication, it was moving into a house designed by this interesting and multi-faceted character that initially stimulated the author to find out more about him and embark upon an intensive period of research. This soon revealed that a number of short articles and booklets about Troyte Griffith had been written over the years, mainly by Catherine Moody, and his name appears frequently in biographies of Edward Elgar, but it seemed appropriate and long overdue for someone to put together a more comprehensive account of his life and his works.

The first chapter is concerned with biographical details about Troyte and his family. Both of his parents came from interesting backgrounds, and his father was a distinguished scientist and teacher. Troyte was the eldest of eleven children who were born between 1864–1878, either in Oxford or, later, in Harrow where their father was a housemaster for many years. After school and university, Troyte eventually came in 1896 to live and work in Malvern, where he remained, unmarried, for the rest of his days.

Troyte was an architect by profession and he designed a number of notable buildings in and around Malvern. In chapter two there is a description of many of these buildings, illustrated by photographs taken by the author and others. Troyte's architectural work was very much in the Arts and Crafts tradition and his houses are generally well built and much appreciated by their owners, although he never quite achieved the level of recognition enjoyed by some of his better-known contemporaries in the early part of the twentieth century.

In addition to being a successful architect, Troyte was also an accomplished painter in watercolours. Most of his pictures were of landscapes or studies of buildings, and several examples of these are shown in chapter three. To further exemplify Troyte's talents as an artist and designer, some of his designs for church interiors and a West End theatre production are also included in this chapter.

Troyte is probably best known outside of Malvern for his long and close friendship with Edward Elgar. Early in the twentieth century, Elgar founded the Malvern Concert Club, as described in chapter four, and, although he was not particularly musical himself, Troyte took on the role of honorary secretary, a post he filled with great distinction for almost forty years, putting together the programmes for one hundred and thirty-nine concerts during this period. The fact that to this day the Concert Club continues to prosper and bring the finest exponents of chamber music to Malvern is a great testament to the foresight and endeavours of both Elgar and Troyte Griffith.

Chapter five gives an account of Troyte's great friendship with Edward Elgar and his family, drawing heavily on correspondence between them from their first meeting in 1896 until 1934. The story is amplified by some notes on Elgar that Troyte wrote after Elgar's death and comments from others, including Elgar's daughter Carice. The two men obviously enjoyed one another's company, sharing an interest in walking or cycling around the countryside, and engaging in animated arguments and discussions. Even when the Elgar family moved away from the Malvern area and Sir Edward, as he now was, became increasingly in demand as his fame grew around the world, they managed to keep in touch until the end. Fittingly, both Alice and Edward Elgar are buried at St Wulstan's Church, Little Malvern, in a grave chosen by Troyte Griffith and beneath a headstone designed by him.

CHAPTER ONE
TROYTE GRIFFITH:
THE MAN AND HIS FAMILY

Arthur Troyte Griffith was born in Oxford on 19 June, 1864. He was the eldest child of George Griffith, MA (1833–1902) and Harriet Dyke Acland Griffith (1838–1921). He lived in Oxford for the first three years of his life, during which time his first two sisters were born, before the family moved to Harrow, where Troyte spent his remaining childhood and adolescence. More will be said about Troyte and his siblings after a few words about his parents.

George Griffith was a distinguished scientist and schoolmaster. His occupation in 1864 was recorded on Troyte's birth certificate as Deputy Professor of Experimental Philosophy at Oxford University but within a short time he was working elsewhere as a schoolmaster. George Griffith was born on 20 October, 1833, at Llangunner, Carmarthen, being the eldest son of the Revd James Griffith, canon of St David's. He was educated at St David's School, from where he won a scholarship to Jesus College, Oxford, taking a first class in natural science in 1856. From 1864–1866 he was a science lecturer at Winchester before, in 1867, he was appointed to teach natural science at Harrow School. He subsequently became housemaster of Druries House in 1887, staying at the school until he retired in 1893. Druries House was originally founded in 1790 as the Abbey but the name was changed to Druries in 1857 in honour of Henry and Ben Drury, father and son, who had been in charge of the house between them for fifty-seven years.

George Griffith was also, for almost forty years, assistant general secretary of the British Association until his death in 1902. In his address to the seventy-second meeting of the British Association that year, the president, Professor James Dewar (later Sir James Dewar) remarked:

> We miss today a figure that has been familiar, conspicuous, and always congenial at the meetings of the British Association during the last forty years. Throughout the greater part of that period Mr George Griffith discharged the onerous and often delicate duties of the assistant general secretary, not only with conscientious thoroughness and great ability, but also with urbanity, tact, and courtesy that endeared him to all. His years sat lightly upon him, and his undiminished alertness and vigour caused his sudden death to come upon us all with a shock of surprise as well as of pain and grief. The British Association owes him a debt of gratitude which must be so fully realised by every regular attender of our meetings that no poor words of mine are needed to quicken your sense of loss, or add to the poignancy of your regret.

Drawing of George Griffith (artist unknown). Photograph of George Griffith.

The sudden death to which the president referred apparently occurred on a train between Baker Street and St John's Wood, on his way home to Harrow.

A very full and interesting obituary for George Griffith was written by Frank K. Beddard and published in the *Harrovian* of 7 June, 1902. As well as pointing out Griffith's considerable abilities and achievements, this piece well illustrates some of the difficulties encountered by the first science teachers in the late nineteenth century:

> There is no object in disguising the fact that from 1867 to the period when the present science schools were built, the study of the natural sciences was not looked upon at Harrow or at any public school with great favour. This was in no way caused by any unwillingness to recognise the educational value of such studies or by anything approaching to narrow-mindedness; it was simply a reflection of current opinion, concentrated and distorted, it may be, as through an imperfect lens by the attitude of the universities and especially by the magnificent conservatism of Oxford. Science offered no practical inducements; in vulgar parlance it led nowhere. The teaching of science being a quite novel procedure, it followed that the facilities for giving instruction were limited.
>
> [Frank Beddard went on to add:] As a lecturer he undoubtedly held the attention of those who had the slightest leaning towards science. His obvious enthusiasm and plainness of exposition did not fail to influence at least some of his hearers; while the willingness with which he devoted half-holidays to the informal instruction was a lesson in itself, quite apart from the value of the technical information imparted. It was precisely the width of Griffith's sympathies and interests in science that rendered him so competent an adviser of boys just beginning to enter upon the flowery and thorny paths of that discipline.

Notwithstanding the above complimentary description of George Griffith's undoubted strengths as a teacher, another contemporary account by J. G. Cotton Minchin in his book *Old Harrow Days,* which was published in 1898, suggests that he did not always manage to keep good order amongst the boys in his class. Minchin writes:

> But what sense of gentlemanly conduct or even honour has the average boy when face to face with a master who had not the faculty of keeping order? I well remember the boys in our 'stinks' class roaring with laughter over some boyish joke. Mr George Griffith was at that moment referring to Sir Isaac Newton. 'I never thought,' he said, 'to live to see the day when English boys would laugh at the illustrious name of Newton.' We boys were no more laughing at Newton than at the great Khan of Tartary. It is needless to add that the rebuke made us roar louder than ever. What barbarians are boys! A thoughtful and gentle master is with them sometimes like a monkish scholar amid the knights in mail of the middle ages.

After retiring from his school appointment, George Griffith continued to work on behalf of the British Association. Some idea of the scope of his wide range of contacts with eminent scientists of the day can be gleaned from the many letters that have been preserved in the Troyte Griffith Collection of Autograph Letters in the archives of the Manchester Central Library. Fortunately for those not living near Manchester, this fascinating collection can also be viewed on microfilm at the Malvern Library.

Troyte's mother (neé Harriet Dyke Acland Troyte) was the second daughter of Sir Arthur Henry Dyke Acland Troyte, Bart. (formerly Acland, 1811–1857) of Huntsham, Devon, who had succeeded to the estates of the Revd Edward Berkeley Troyte and took the surname and arms of Troyte by royal licence in 1852. It was a condition of his inheritance that Arthur Acland should take the name of Troyte, so the rather uncommon middle name given to his eldest son, by which he was usually known, originated from his mother's family. This same middle name was also given to several of the other Griffith children.

Apart from other achievements, Troyte's maternal grandfather, Arthur H. D. Troyte, was the composer of several chants and hymn tunes, including *Troyte's Chant No. 1, Troyte's Chant No. 2* and *Lonsdale,* more details of which can be found on the website www.hymnary.org. Several members of the Troyte family in Huntsham were involved with bell ringing and further details of their history can be found on the website of the Troyte Ringing Centre at www.troyteringingcentre.org.uk/huntsham_history.htm.

Harriet married George Griffith in 1863 and went on to produce eleven children over the following fifteen years, one of whom, Agnes Acland Griffith, was born in 1868 and died the same year.

Of the children who survived the first year of life, Troyte had four brothers (Charles, Edward, Herbert and John) and five sisters (Frances, Sarah, Ethel, Gertrude and Lilian), as shown in the family tree. In the Census of 1891, as well as this large family, the Griffith household in Harrow is also shown to include one visitor and eight servants (butler, two footmen, cook, kitchen maid, scullery maid, two housemaids). Although this sounds like rather a houseful to modern ears, such numbers of servants would not have been unusual at this time for a man of George Griffith's status.

Troyte was a pupil at Harrow School from September 1877 until the summer of 1883. At school he was apparently known by the nickname of 'Tusker' because of the appearance of his teeth, a physical characteristic referred to many years later by George Bernard Shaw when he asked Victor Moody, 'Has Troyte Griffith still got those awful teeth?'

Troyte's teeth are not actually shown in most of the photographs that are currently available, apart from the one of him apparently supporting his four younger brothers on his shoulders, so it is rather difficult to make a professional assessment of the state of his dentition.

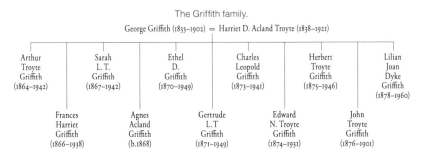

The Griffith family.

George Griffith (1833–1902) = Harriet D. Acland Troyte (1838–1921)

Arthur Troyte Griffith (1864–1942)	Sarah L.T. Griffith (1867–1942)	Ethel D. Griffith (1870–1949)	Charles Leopold Griffith (1873–1941)	Herbert Troyte Griffith (1875–1946)	Lilian Joan Dyke Griffith (1878–1960)
Frances Harriet Griffith (1866–1938)	Agnes Acland Griffith (b.1868)	Gertrude L.T Griffith (1871–1949)	Edward N. Troyte Griffith (1874–1931)	John Troyte Griffith (1876–1901)	

The Griffith brothers, Arthur Troyte Griffith is on the extreme right.

Above: drawing of Harriet Griffith.
Right: the Griffith brothers on a ladder,
from the top: John, Herbert,
Edward, Charles Leopold, and Arthur.

There is very little available information about Troyte's time at school. The Harrow School archives reveal only that he resided in a small boarding house but, unfortunately, the records do not give any more detail about which one. As a result, it is not possible to state with any certainty whether he belonged to Druries or one of the other dozen or so houses. The headmaster during the whole of Troyte's period at Harrow School was the Revd Henry Montagu Butler, who occupied the post from 1860–1885, but how much contact Troyte may have had with him is unknown.

Contemporary accounts of life at Harrow School in the nineteenth century can be found in the aforementioned book by Minchin and in Hugh Russell at Harrow: *A Sketch of School Life by an Old Harrovian*, published 1880. Fagging was certainly one of the traditions still in operation in Troyte's time and the school had developed quite an extensive vocabulary of words and expressions that were peculiar to Harrow. However, it is impossible to say which of the various traditions, punishments and pleasures described in these books were actually experienced by Troyte. Did he ever feel the pain of the birch, enjoy singing lustily the school song 'Forty Years On', attend the annual Eton versus Harrow match at Lord's, enjoy playing cricket and 'footer', or become a school monitor? Alas, we shall probably never know the answers to such questions.

Troyte's younger brothers evidently attended other schools, two of them (Herbert and John) went to Haileybury, even though their father was a master at Harrow.

Troyte matriculated on 27 October, 1883 at Oxford where he became a student at Oriel College. For reasons that are not entirely clear, he appears to have studied for an ordinary rather than an honours degree, eventually taking his BA in December, 1887. Catherine Moody tried to find out more about Troyte's academic career at Oxford through correspondence with Dr Lionel Clowes of Magdalene College during 1979. According to Dr Clowes, it was not that uncommon for undergraduates to opt for a pass degree rather than an honours degree in Victorian times. Troyte evidently passed examinations in 'Elements of Political Economy', and in 'Geometry, including Geometrical Trigonometry' in the Michaelmas Term of 1885. In the Trinity Term of 1886 he passed in 'Greek and Latin, including Greek philosophy and ancient history' for which subjects the set books were Aristotle's *Ethics* and Tacitus's *Annals*. Lionel Clowes did not regard this as a very onerous programme of study and suggested that Troyte may have spent his time profitably doing other things that were not examined. He did not subsequently take his MA, for which he would have been eligible seven years after matriculation, perhaps because he did not consider it to be worth the extra fuss and expense required to obtain a degree that was not essential for his chosen career as an architect.

Not very much is known about how Troyte spent his undergraduate days at Oxford, but many years later his contemporary M. L. Banks recorded the following in his obituary in the *Malvern Gazette:*

> The writer well remembers meeting Arthur Troyte Griffith in the rooms of a mutual friend. He lived the life of a quiet, studious scholar, but though not an athlete, he was on easy terms of friendship with the best set at Oriel – a college where skill at games counted a great deal. Troyte cared little for politics, sport or society, a library was dukedom enough. On music, art and architecture he held strong, independent views and would stick to his point, even though it were professionally to his own hindrance.

It is unfortunate that there do not appear to be any other contemporary records of Troyte's time at Oxford or of what sort of company he kept. However, it is known that he played chess for his college and for the university whilst he was at Oxford, an interest that he actively pursued in later years in Malvern.

There is rather a pronounced gap in available information about Troyte's life between graduation from Oxford and his arrival in Malvern in 1896, during which period he must have developed much of his knowledge and skill as a draughtsman and architect. In a letter from his nephew, Rennie Bere (son of Troyte's sister Sarah) to Catherine Moody, it is suggested that Troyte spent a year or two 'foot loose' on the continent. He may well have visited an uncle, the Revd R. H. Acland Troyte, who lived in Pau in the French Pyrenees. Many years later, Catherine Moody unearthed a magazine illustration in the *Studio* of 1910 which shows an altar frontal for St Andrew's Anglican Church in Pau designed by Troyte, as described in more detail later.

Troyte was awarded the Aldenwinkle Studentship for 1897 by the Royal Institute of British Architects (RIBA) on the basis of reports and drawings submitted to the council. The award was to allow for travel in Spain for a period of not less than eight weeks. According to Catherine Moody, Troyte also took up a scholarship to study the architecture of France and Spain in 1904. It appears that the very frugal funding of the scholarship made it necessary for him to travel by train at night so that he could avoid the cost of overnight accommodation. The whereabouts of the many sketchbooks and studies arising from this expedition, as reported in correspondence from Rennie Bere, are not known.

Troyte came to Malvern in 1896 and started working for the firm of architects Nevinson and Newton, whose offices were situated in the Priory Gateway. Edward Bonney Nevinson (1867–1959), the architect, was the brother of the cellist Basil George Nevinson, a friend of Edward Elgar, who played chamber music with the composer and became the subject of *Enigma Variation* no. XII ('B.G.N.'). A third member of the family, their uncle Edward Henry Nevinson, was a solicitor who also worked at Priory Gateway, for the firm Nevinson and Barlow.

Troyte was involved with the Malvern Chess Club from its inaugural meeting on 28 February, 1899, at which he was elected secretary and treasurer. He was evidently a fine player who dominated the club for many years. According to Charles Gray (who died in 1995), in a brief history of the club written many years after Troyte's death, his combative skill in chess was impressive and his games seldom reached an end game. He represented Worcestershire on occasions and, at Malvern, was sometimes asked to play simultaneous matches against several other members of the club, winning most of them. In 1931, on the death of fellow founder member Hugh Bennett, Troyte Griffith was elected to replace him as president of the Malvern Chess Club, but only agreed to hold the position for a year. He continued to be a strong player until his death in 1942, winning the Malvern Chess Club Championship in 1938–1939.

Malvern Chess Club Championship Cup. The inscription reads: '1938/9 Championship, A Troyte Griffith'.

Physically, Troyte was a tall, thin figure who earned the nickname of the 'Giddy Ninepin' from his friend Edward Elgar. According to Carice Elgar Blake's obituary in the *Musical Times,* he bore a strong facial resemblance to Robert Louis Stevenson. Certainly, the two men seem from photographic evidence to have sported similar moustaches and hairstyles.

A number of pictures of Troyte Griffith exist, including photographs and the fine sketch by Illingworth Varley, which has been used in several other publications. Perhaps the best known image is the drawing by Victor Moody, showing Troyte striding along in his characteristic knee breeches, stockings and Norfolk jacket. Rennie Bere wrote to Catherine Moody saying, 'Your father's sketch was a marvellously good likeness and absolutely typical of the "Uncle Arty" of my youth.' This is particularly remarkable, considering that the sketch was drawn from memory some thirty-five years after Troyte's death.

Troyte lived for many years in a house at Lower Wyche called Fair View, described by Catherine Moody as '… built of Malvern stone with deep brick quoins, in the cottagey vernacular building of the pre-nineteenth century.' The property, built in 1815, had at one time been an inn called The Rose and Crown and was also sometimes referred to as Golf View. He was cared for there by a housekeeper, Mrs Mary Ann Williams, and her daughter, Dorothy; in his will, he stipulated that Mrs Williams should be allowed to continue to live in the house after his death for her remaining days. It was evidently a quiet and well-ordered household, his needs being simple and regular.

Troyte appears to have been somewhat loath to accept invitations in the afternoons for fear of missing his regular tea at home, unless, perhaps, the invitation came from the Elgar family. This slight

Photograph of Robert Louis Stevenson.   Photograph of Arthur Troyte Griffith.

Sketch of Arthur Troyte Griffith   Drawing of Arthur Troyte Griffith
by Illingworth Varley.   by Victor Hume Moody.

difficulty over tea arrangements is amusingly recounted by Catherine Moody in an article she wrote for the *Elgar Society Journal* in 1999. In the same piece, she quotes her friend Margaret Hamand, daughter of organist and choirmaster Dr Louis Hamand, who describes Troyte's 'spare and energetic figure' as follows:

> Dressed in the Norfolk jacket, knee breeches and stockings, he was always in action, walking or riding his famous bicycle. His conversation was equally spare. He only uttered when it was necessary, never bolstering up a situation with social chitchat.

Functional design was the key to his architecture and to his life. His general demeanour could evidently be somewhat alarming to a young girl until 'something amused him, when his whole face crumpled up in spluttering and endearing laughter.'

Not much is known about Troyte's relationship with other people, apart from his great friendship with Edward Elgar, although from some accounts he does not always seem to have been very comfortable with female company. He remained a bachelor throughout his life and there are no records of any romantic attachments.

He was obviously a well-read and cultivated man, not conspicuously active in local or national politics, although there is correspondence which suggests that he was considered by some to lean towards socialism.

In a letter to Kevin Allen, dated 6 September, 1994, Robert Bartleet (son of Canon Hubert Humphrey Middlemore Bartleet, vicar of Malvern Priory from 1924–1947) wrote:

> Troyte Griffith I met when I was very young and he came to lunch. I remember my mother saying he was a brilliant architect and a very nice man, it was a pity he was a socialist.
>
> He was a member of that group of early socialists which contained the Webbs, Bernard Shaw and William Morris.

This connection with socialism was confirmed recently by the discovery that Troyte was a paid-up subscriber to the Fabian Society from 1901–1941, only resigning the year before his death. The Fabian Society was founded on 4 January, 1884 when some friends of the young solicitor, Edward Pease, met at the London home of George Bernard Shaw to formulate the terms of reference for a 'Fellowship of the New Life.' It is not known exactly how Troyte became involved with the Fabians or whether he attended any of their meetings.

Troyte evidently did not have much faith in modern, new-fangled inventions. He did not have a telephone in his office and did not normally use a typewriter for correspondence, preferring to write all his letters in his own hand. Fortunately for historians and biographers, Troyte's handwriting was extremely clear and easy to read, unlike that of Edward Elgar.

One of Catherine Moody's contacts, Mrs Hughes, whose father lived two doors away from Fair View, recalled:

> My early memories of Troyte Griffith are not so much of the man but of his bicycle! Troyte was a tall man and his bicycle was tall with the saddle consisting of a strong, green net, having one end attached to the handle bars, quite different from the normal saddle. [She continued,] He always seemed to be wearing the same clothes – a cloth hat and a cloak which I understood he had bought in Germany.'

As remarked by Catherine, the bicycle does not sound as if it was very comfortable. It was almost certainly a Pederson or Dursley Pederson model which had been developed by the Danish inventor Mikael Pederson and was produced in the English town of Dursley from about 1894. The Pederson bicycles all featured a distinctive hammock-style seat.

As will be discussed in more detail in a later chapter, Troyte became a close friend of Edward Elgar soon after he moved to Malvern. He must have been quite distressed when Elgar died in 1934 as their friendship had become an important part of his life. Although they were able to meet less often after Edward moved away from Malvern, particularly whilst the Elgars lived in London, the two men had maintained contact with one another by regular postal correspondence over many years.

Troyte Griffith died on 17 January, 1942, after a short illness described as 'heart failure'. As reported in the *Malvern Gazette* of 24 January, the funeral took place on Wednesday, 21 January, at All Saints Church, Malvern Wells, with the vicar of the Wyche, the Revd B. A. Townsend, officiating. Troyte's youngest sisters, Gertrude and Lilian Griffith, were amongst the chief mourners, but several other

Fair View, Troyte Griffith's house in Malvern Wells.

members of the family were unable to be present, as was Elgar's daughter, Mrs Carice Elgar Blake. However, Carice did write an obituary for the *Musical Times,* published in February, 1942, which is reproduced in full below with the kind permission of the editor:

> Arthur Troyte Griffith, 'Troyte', whose death occurred on 17 January, after a very short illness, was the eldest son of George Griffith, MA, first science master and housemaster at Harrow

School, and Harriet Dyke Griffith. He was educated at Harrow and Oxford University.

By profession an architect, he came to Malvern in 1896, where he settled, and he became responsible for many beautiful buildings in the county, including the Wyche church, where his funeral was held. The friendship with Elgar began very soon after he came to Malvern, and lasted until Elgar's death in 1934. He was a constant visitor to Elgar's home in Malvern, and later in Hereford and Hampstead; and no assembly for a great event, such as a first performance of one of Elgar's works, or a Three Choirs Festival, was complete without him. He had a great knowledge of literature, English and French, and the classics; the discussions and friendly arguments between the two men were almost endless. He was always to the fore in the solutions of Torquemada's crossword puzzles in later days. Elgar aroused his interest in music, of which he had little knowledge, and he was immortalized in the 'Variations'. Elgar's own notes on this Variation explain that it represented an attempt to teach Troyte the rudiments of piano playing, and the teacher's impatient despair. Though not successful as a performer, Troyte became secretary and treasurer of the Malvern Concert Club, founded by Elgar in 1902, for which such world-famed artists as Elena Gerhardt and the Brodsky Quartet frequently performed. Elgar presented him with a gold watch after twenty-one years of devoted service to the club. Just before his death, he had completed the arrangements for the concerts for 1942. He was well known as an artist in water-colour. Worcester Cathedral, Birchwood, Upton-upon-Severn, the garden of Craeg Lea and many places intimately associated with Elgar are among his sketches. He was very thin and tall, which earned him Elgar's nickname of the 'Ninepin', and bore a strong facial resemblance to Robert Louis Stevenson.

Troyte's last remaining sibling was his youngest sister, Lilian Griffith, who died in 1960. She was one of the two executrixes and main beneficiaries of his estate, together with her sister Gertrude, who predeceased her in 1949. No pictures of Gertrude have been discovered but Lilian at the age of about seventy-one can be seen below in a picture taken by Jerrold Northrop Moore, in 1959, in the front garden of her home in Wellington, Somerset. Neither of these sisters ever married.

Troyte was buried in a simple grave in the cemetery at Malvern Wells.

Having described in outline Troyte's life from birth to death, the chapters which follow will explore in more detail some aspects of his work as an architect, his artistic talents and his friendship with Edward Elgar.

Lilian Griffith outside her house in Wellington, Somerset, in 1959.

Troyte Griffith's grave in Malvern Wells cemetery.

Malvern Wells cemetery: Troyte Griffith's grave is
towards the end of the path, on the right past the tree.

CHAPTER TWO
TROYTE GRIFFITH:
THE ARCHITECT

PREAMBLE

Although Troyte Griffith worked in Malvern for many years as a successful architect, it has proved difficult to find any information about his formal training. He evidently did not acquire recognised professional qualifications from the Royal Institute of British Architects (RIBA), despite winning an award from that august institution. It is known that he travelled around Europe after graduating from Oxford University in 1887, especially in Spain and France, studying buildings, drawing and painting, but details of his activities during this period are scanty. In the census of 1891 he is shown as being a resident at his parents' address in Harrow and his profession is listed as 'architect', so it seems probable that he must have worked as a pupil or assistant in an architect's office in the local area, or, perhaps, some other part of London.

The London-based firm of architects, Nevinson and Newton, whose main office was at 7 Staple Inn, Holborn, had established a branch office in the Priory Gateway, Malvern, in 1894. Edward Bonney Nevinson was born in Leicester in 1858 and died in London in 1928. He was educated at Shrewsbury School and became an Associate of the RIBA in January, 1882. Nevinson's partner, John Floyd Newton, was born in 1859, went to Haileybury School, as did Troyte's brothers Herbert and John Griffith, where he excelled at cricket. He also became ARIBA in 1882 and, like Nevinson, worked for a time for James Piers St Aubyn before they set up their own practice. He resigned from the RIBA in 1928 and died in 1945.

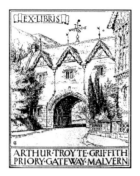

ARTHUR·TROYTE·GRIFFITH
PRIORY·GATEWAY·MALVERN

Troyte Griffith's bookplate
showing the Priory Gateway.

Troyte joined Nevinson and Newton as an architectural assistant in 1896 and was involved in the design and construction of a number of buildings whilst working for them, most notably All Saints Church at the Wyche. A few years after this church had been consecrated in 1903, Nevinson and Newton ceased operating in Malvern and from 1908 Troyte took over their offices in his own name, according to the entry for 'architects' in Stevens Annual for that year, although some sources indicate that he was in charge from about 1906. He practised as an architect from the Priory Gateway until 1935, at which point he moved to an office nearby at Prior's Croft in Grange Road, from where he worked until his death in 1942.

In the archives of the Malvern Priory, there is a detailed drawing of the ground plan of the church signed by Troyte Griffith and dated 1896. One may perhaps speculate that he could have been given this task when he first started working for Nevinson and Newton as an early test of his skills as a draughtsman, although he may simply have done it because of his own keen interest in church architecture.

In the sections which follow, known examples of Troyte's architectural work will be described, illustrating the many significant contributions he made to the built environment of Malvern over his long career. There are almost certainly other buildings designed by Troyte Griffith in and around Malvern that have not been included in this review, and the author would be interested to receive details of any other notable buildings which should be added to the list of his works for future reference.

THE TOPOSCOPE

Situated on the summit of the Worcestershire Beacon, high on the Malvern Hills, the Toposcope is probably the most conspicuous and best known of Troyte's designs. Also known as 'the Indicator', this structure consists of an engraved circular map showing the main geographical features of the surrounding countryside, mounted on a short column which is set on a granite plinth. It was erected in 1899, two years after the Diamond Jubilee, although the inscription on the side states 'Erected in Commemoration of the Sixtieth Year of Queen Victoria's Reign 1897.' However, the date of the inauguration did take place on the anniversary of the Queen's accession (which occurred on 20 June, 1837). The original idea was suggested by the vicar of Malvern at the time, the Revd Raymond P. Pelly. The project was over seen by an Indicator Committee (chaired by Mr H. D. Acland) and the Toposcope was officially inaugurated with great ceremony on Tuesday, 20 June, before a large gathering of prominent Malvern citizens who had ascended the hill to witness the event.

A detailed report of the inauguration, in the *Malvern Advertiser* of Saturday, 24 June, 1899, describes how the vicar and four other clergy, together with the Priory Church Choir, all in cassocks and surplices, assembled at St Anne's Well, and after singing a hymn, processed with banner and cross to the summit, where a dedication service was conducted. This included the singing of the Apostles Creed, Preces and Responses, the Lord's Prayer, the Benedicite and two hymns, and appropriate prayers and collects were intoned by the vicar. It was evidently quite an elaborate service for an open-air event and one hopes that it was not too windy for the vicar and choir to be heard.

As reported in the newspaper 'At this juncture a very unexpected incident occurred. A gentleman named Mr Boobyer, a visitor, called out loudly (as he did so pointing to the cross and banner): "In the name of God I denounce these Popish symbols being used in a service like this. It is a disgrace to a Protestant country." No response was made, and the denunciator quietly left.'

Following this slight disturbance, the Indicator was unveiled by Mrs Dixey, wife of Dr Dixey, and various speeches were made, with thanks being given to the designer, Mr A. T. Griffith, who 'had been unfailing in his desire to get the Indicator as perfect as possible.' After a few more well-chosen words, the official ceremony was concluded with the singing of the national anthem, whereupon those present crowded round to inspect the Indicator more closely.

The same newspaper article also included a lengthy and detailed description of the Indicator, provided by Troyte Griffith. In this, he comments that:

> The plate of the Malvern Indicator consists of two distinct portions. In the central circle is an outline map with Malvern as the centre and a radius of sixty-seven miles, sufficient to include the most distant points that have been absolutely identified from the Beacon. The outer rim contains a panoramic view or diagram of what can be actually seen on a clear day, and, as stated in a note on the plate, the names of those places that have been observed with certainty have been engraved in capitals, those that cannot be seen, or are doubtful, in italics.

He went on to explain that it was practically certain that fifteen counties had been seen from the Beacon, whilst sightings of about seven others were less certain. After some explanation of the technical difficulties experienced during the construction and erection of the Indicator, he acknowledged by name the individuals who were involved. He added that copies of the engraved plate were available for sale in the town (as they are still today), with money derived from this source being devoted to a fund for cleaning the Indicator, as necessary.

Sadly, in February 2000, the engraved brass plate from the Toposcope was stolen, thus depriving walkers on the Malvern Hills the pleasure of enjoying a historic landmark that had been in place for more than a century. Fortunately, following an anonymous tip-off, the plate was eventually recovered by police in Walsall in December, 2001, and returned to the Malvern Hills Conservators. Since then, two copies of the plate have been made and one of these has been installed on the plinth on the summit of the Worcestershire Beacon. At the same time, a new protective glass cover was commissioned with improved properties to reduce water condensation and preserve clear visibility of the map beneath. The original plate is now kept by the Conservators, hopefully safe from the attention of any more would-be thieves.

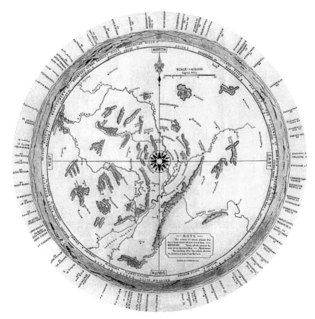

An illustration of the plate on top of the Toposcope illustrating the local landmarks that can be seen in different directions from the Worcestershire Beacon.

The Toposcope on the Worcestershire Beacon.

ALL SAINTS CHURCH,
LOWER WYCHE, MALVERN WELLS

Whilst working for the firm of Nevinson and Newton, Troyte was heavily involved in the design and building of All Saints Church at Lower Wyche, close to his own home Fair View, in Malvern Wells. According to the memorial plaque erected on the inside of the church years after its completion, he was the architect, although credit should perhaps more properly be given to the parent firm. According to Brooks and Pevsner in *The Buildings of England: Worcestershire* (2007), the church was built in 1902–1903 by A. Troyte Griffith (of Nevinson and Newton).

As described by Brooks and Pevsner, the church was built against the hillside, rock-faced with ashlar (dressed Malvern stone) and Hereford brick dressings. There is a nave and chancel, with a north vestry and a curved apse at the east end, on the exterior wall of which is a niche containing a carved stone figure of St George, given in memory of Mr Malcolm Cathcart, which was added in 1934. On the south-west there is a porch and on the roof, above the chancel arch, is an oak bellcote with a small copper-covered flèche (spire). The windows are mostly lancets (tall, narrow and pointed, in Gothic style).

The interior of the church is faced with brick, the windows recessed within large receiving arches, and there is an arch-braced roof and a wide moulded stone chancel arch. The builder was Mr W. Porter and the stonework was carried out by Mr T. Jones. It is reported that Troyte was meticulous in his supervision of the building and that he personally selected every piece of Malvern stone from the quarry for all the exterior surfaces.

There is some excellent stained glass by Henry Payne (1868–1940) of the Bromsgrove Guild, who is well-known for his work at Madresfield Court and a set of panels in the Houses of Parliament. The glass includes the east window in the apse (1904), the apostles window in the south chancel (1905), and further examples in the south nave (1918) and the north nave (1937 – probably completed by his son, Edward Payne, according to Brooks and Pevsner).

One particularly notable feature is the carved and gilded wood reredos above the altar. As recorded by Mr E. W. Wilmott, writing

in the *All Saints Parish News Sheet* of August, 1978, this was designed
by Troyte Griffith in 1905, two years after the church was opened; the
painting was carried out by Henry Payne. The commissioning of the
reredos evidently came about thanks to a gift from someone referred
to as 'Sister Laura' in 1905, 'in memory of her two brothers and two
sisters,' but the full identity of the donor is not recorded.

Several interesting additional facts about All Saints Church are
revealed in the *Brief History* written by Diana Medley and Cliff Prosser
in January, 2000. When the need for a new church in Malvern Wells
became apparent because of the increase in the number of houses in
the area at the end of the nineteenth century, concerted efforts were
made to raise funds for the project. Lady Emily Foley was amongst
the donors and, in January 1900, her substantial gift was apparently
her last public benefaction. Once sufficient funds had been raised, the
foundation stone was laid on 3 November, 1902, by Lettice, Countess
Beauchamp. This stone, with its inscription, can still be seen on the
outside wall of the apse, beneath the figure of St George, at the east
end of the church.

The new church was consecrated on 19 November, 1903, by the
bishop of Worcester, Dr Charles Gore, assisted by the Revd Canon
R. P. Pelly, vicar of Malvern. A full account of proceedings was reported
in the *Malvern News* of 21 November, 1903 and a slightly shorter version
appeared in the *Malvern Gazette* of the same date.

From 1899–1904, Troyte Griffith's great friend, Edward Elgar, lived
nearby in Wells Road at Craeg Lea. He wrote from here to August
Jaeger (now best remembered as 'Nimrod' in the *Enigma Variations*)
on 25 January, 1903, that 'Troyte is architecting this Church here and
wants to call it "the Holy Apostles" and wants me to go and write in
the crypt so as to give it, or imbibe from it, local colour.' He enclosed
a photograph of the foundations of the church which was then under
construction just to the north of Craeg Lea. In some notes that Troyte
wrote many years later, he commented further on background to the
naming of the church:

> I was building a church about one hundred yards from Craeg
> Lea at the time, and when it was finished I told Elgar that I

All Saints Church, Lower Wyche,
Malvern Wells, east end.

All Saints Church, Lower Wyche,
Malvern Wells, south side.

The altar and reredos at All Saints Church, reredos designed by
Troyte Griffith and painted by Henry Payne in 1905.

thought of suggesting to the Vicar that it should be dedicated to the Apostles. This rather pleased Elgar and he said, 'Well, if they do I will deposit my full score manuscript in the church, but you mustn't tell Canon Pelly.' However, the church was dedicated to All Saints. When I told Elgar, he said 'That's just like the Church of England. You have got no saints of your own so you grab the whole lot at one fell swoop.

All Saints Church, south-western aspect.

There has been some controversy in the past over who should claim the credit for the design of All Saints Church, but as is clear from the earlier quotation from Pevsner, the church was built under the direction of Troyte Griffith whilst he was working for Nevinson and Newton. The church certainly stands as a proud monument of Troyte's skill as an architect.

RESEARCH INTO THE
IDENTITY OF TROYTE'S HOUSES

As a special Silver Jubilee Year Project, the Malvern Architectural Society decided to undertake the task of recording as much as possible of the life and work of Troyte Griffith, before all first-hand memories faded away completely. As part of this process, a letter from Catherine Moody was published in the *Malvern Gazette* on 13 January, 1977 requesting that any readers 'who might live in a house designed wholly or partly by Arthur Troyte Griffith, or might have any information about him, would communicate with me.' Catherine was at the time chairman of the Architectural Society, the president was the architect Michael Peach, RIBA, and the secretary was Mr E. W. Wilmott, who lived at Greyroofs in Peachfield Road and was a churchwarden at the nearby All Saints Church. This letter in the local newspaper led to a considerable amount of private correspondence with Catherine which yielded much additional background information about Troyte Griffith.

Further publicity for this project was achieved by an article in the *Malvern Gazette Special Jubilee Supplement* of 2 June, 1977 on 'Discovering Arthur Troyte Griffith: Search for an Enigmatic Character,' written by Catherine Moody. Accompanying this article were pictures of the Toposcope on the Worcestershire Beacon (from an old postcard), a photograph of Troyte Griffith with Mr Thomas Jones and a group of masons in 1916, and the reredos at All Saints Church, Lower Wyche.

An important part of the research undertaken in 1977 by members of the Malvern Architectural Society was to examine the archives of the Malvern Hills District Council planning department, access to which was enabled by the planning officer, Mr J. D. Wallis. From the Malvern Urban District Council's Register of Plans 1883–1934, they were able to compile a list of building projects with which Troyte Griffith, or his employers Nevinson and Newton in the early years, had been involved. The hand-written notes made at the time by Catherine Moody still provide a most valuable source of reference.

In 1977 Catherine Moody also produced her delightful small booklet about Arthur Troyte Griffith entitled *A Malvern Eccentric*. This was published in a limited edition of sixty copies by Malvern Hills College (of which Catherine was Head at the time), hand set at the college and printed on special mould-made paper from St Cuthbert's Mill, Wookey Hole. At the end of this booklet, as examples of his work, is a list of eight of the houses then known to be designed by Troyte, together with the reredos at All Saints Church.

Further recollections of Troyte Griffith and his work were presented at the November meeting of the Malvern Architectural Society and are described in some detail in the *Malvern Gazette* of 17 November, 1977. This must have been a particularly interesting occasion as it included reminiscences from several individuals who had actually known Troyte personally, as well as a display of photographs, watercolours and other relevant material.

Some of the fruits of the labours of the Malvern Architectural Society's researches were presented in the form of two lectures about Troyte Griffith during the 1978 Fringe Festival. These were given on Sunday, 4 June, and Friday, 9 June, at the Montrose Hotel in Graham Road by Michael Peach (president) and Catherine Moody (chairman), with an entrance fee of forty pence for each lecture. As stated in a flyer for the lectures:

> The Malvern Architectural Society has been engaged upon research into the life and work of Arthur Troyte Griffith and has recovered many new facts and has also discovered many of his buildings and is in the process of making a full assessment of his work.

As reported in the *Malvern Gazette* on 8 June, 1978, Michael Peach said in his lecture; 'The main thing to remember about the Malvern architect Troyte Griffith is that he built well.' He went on to review several examples of Troyte's work from his earliest days with Nevinson and Newton onwards, commenting that, 'By 1916 he was sufficiently well-established to be asked to design the Pickersleigh Road School' and went on to remark that his 1933 design for The Orchard in Peachfield Road was '... modern enough to have two bathrooms,' which seems a far cry from present-day expectations of house buyers. The following week, in the *Malvern Gazette* of 15 June, there is a brief report on Catherine Moody's lecture. The colour slides used to illustrate these two lectures, which include photographs of many of Troyte's buildings and examples of his watercolour paintings, are now in the author's collection of Griffith memorabilia.

Sadly, the Malvern Architectural Society no longer exists, but interest in the heritage and architecture of the local area is these days maintained by the very active Malvern Civic Society.

KNOWN HOUSES BY TROYTE GRIFFITH

There are at least seventeen private houses in and around Malvern that are thought to have been designed by Troyte Griffith between 1901 and 1939, plus a few others for which confirmation of his involvement is currently lacking. In addition to designing complete buildings, he was sometimes commissioned to plan extensions and alterations to existing structures, such as 'motor sheds' or garages. There may well be further examples of his work in the area, about which the author is unaware but would be happy to learn of and add to the list of works attributed to Troyte.

Several of the houses were described in a series of two articles by Melanie Peterson in the *Malvern Gazette* of 13 and 20 July, 1978. The author of these articles was clearly very well informed by Catherine Moody, from whom a number of significant quotations were printed, in addition to reproductions of Victor Moody's drawing of Troyte Griffith and a pastel drawing by Catherine Moody of the drawing room of The Orchard in Peachfield Road. In one of the quoted passages, Catherine says:

'He was the inheritor of a new simplicity and style started in this country by Voysey, his contemporary, which found its full expression in the substantial country houses he designed in the Malvern/Colwall area. Working at the same time as Frank Lloyd Wright and Le Corbusier, Troyte Griffith shared the same love of simplicity that typifies Wright's best-known domestic architecture, though his houses were neither as close to nature as the American's nor as avant-garde as Corbusier's.

Many of Troyte's houses have been altered and modernised over the years and some of the original features may have been lost, but they still retain the feeling of spaciousness, good proportions and practicability that is so characteristic of his designs for domestic accommodation. Most of them remain in single family occupation, for which they were intended, rather than being split up into smaller units as is the case with some of the larger Victorian houses in Malvern.

As pointed out by Catherine Moody, Troyte's work is almost devoid of an instantly recognisable style, in contrast to that of a better-known contemporary architect, whom he clearly admired, C. F. A. Voysey (1857–1941). Like Voysey, Troyte was probably influenced by William Morris and the Arts and Crafts movement, but he did not apparently venture into the design of furniture, wallpaper and the full range of other interior features of his houses. Possible exceptions to this notion are Troyte's designs for staircases and the brick-built fireplace surrounds that are seen in several of the properties. In general, the plans are simple, functional, well-proportioned and aesthetically pleasing, but without ever appearing particularly opulent or with exaggerated and fussy details. What does distinguish several of the larger houses is their splendid position, with large gardens and magnificent views, with good examples on both the east and west sides of the Malvern Hills.

The author has managed to visit many of the known Troyte Griffith houses, thanks to the kindness of the current owners, and most of them are illustrated in the following section.

St Mabyn's (Holmside) and Winterholme

The first examples are a pair of semi-detached houses in Worcester Road, completed in 1903 whilst Troyte was still employed by Nevinson and Newton. These houses, St Mabyn's (originally Holmside) and Winterholme, are of quite an unusual design, being built on four floors with a mansard roof and twin gables, as well as a bridge from the road to the front entrance. Troyte produced an interesting watercolour sketch of the building. This picture used to be in the possession of Mr J. A. Tudge, who had worked as a manager for the builder, W. James, later becoming a director, and he lent it to Catherine Moody to illustrate one of her 1978 lectures. It would appear that a certain degree of 'artistic licence' was exercised whilst illustrating the immediate surroundings of the houses. Interesting and impressive as they are, it cannot be said that these particular houses are very typical of the designs that Troyte Griffith subsequently produced during his professional career.

There is an interesting wartime story about St Mabyn's recounted by John Ferris, who used to live there with his parents, which was published in 2003 in the book *Malvern Voices: Wartime, an Oral History* (edited by

Sketch by Troyte Griffith of houses on Worcester Road, Malvern.

Gill Holt). As a young boy, John's bedroom was on the fourth floor of the house, from which one night he spotted flashing lights in the distance during the blackout. After he had ingeniously located approximately where the lights were coming from (on a small hill near Guarlford) and alerted the police, the spy was eventually apprehended. He was caught red-handed on the way down the hill, complete with lighting equipment, as he returned from sending signals to a German plane.

St Mabyn's, Worcester Road, Malvern.   Winterholme, Worcester Road, Malvern.

Greyroofs

A fine, large house in Peachfield Road, Greyroofs, was completed in 1909. It was originally built for a wealthy German count who lived in London with his English wife and family before moving to Malvern. After a few changes in ownership, in 1952 the house was bought by Captain L. C. Lomas who was then the Worcestershire county architect. Sometime later the house was converted into two separate residences, one half being lived in by Lomas's deputy, Donald Sharpe, and to the present day it remains in this sub-divided configuration. In the 1970s, Sharpe's half of Greyroofs was bought by Major E. W. Wilmott, who became secretary of the Malvern Architectural Society and was also churchwarden at All Saints Church, as mentioned previously. Willy Wilmott, who, together with Catherine Moody and other members of the Architectural Society, was largely responsible for the great revival of interest in Troyte Griffith's work in the late 1970s, died in 1991 and his widow moved to a new address in London a few years later.

One unsolved mystery about Greyroofs is the often repeated statement that it was chosen as the *Country Life* House of the Year in 1910. This observation was made on several occasions by Catherine Moody in her various writings about Troyte Griffith and has also been mentioned in the local newspaper, but all attempts to verify this award have so far drawn a blank. Disappointingly, staff at *Country Life* can find no record of Greyroofs being featured in their magazine. It would be interesting to learn if there was some other architectural award made for the house in 1910, perhaps by another magazine or some other organization?

Greyroofs, Peachfield Road, the rear of the house viewed from the garden.

The house is built on a generous scale and, as illustrated, has an interesting roof formation. Like many of Troyte's larger houses, it is positioned on a fine plot with a good-sized garden, although the original beauty and tranquillity of the situation has been threatened severely by adjacent building developments. Internally, in common with other houses, it has high ceilings and a simple, but visually pleasing, wooden staircase.

Greyroofs, Peachfield Road, front aspect.

The Orchard

Not far from Greyroofs, a little lower down Peachfield Road, is another very fine example of Troyte's work, known as The Orchard. It was built originally for Miss Leigh, who was the daughter of Mrs Leigh, the owner of Greyroofs. This property is set back some distance from the road, approached from a small lane, so it is quite easily missed by the casual passer-by. It is particularly unusual because of the distinctive green roof tiles and, like many of Troyte's larger houses, has a splendid garden. It was built in 1931 and is another example where copies of the original plans and a watercolour sketch of the building have been preserved. Like several other houses, The Orchard has a simple, but visually pleasing, wooden staircase and brick fireplaces. As pointed out by Catherine Moody in a talk given in 1978, this house shows that Troyte Griffith had by this time fully developed his own particular quality of domestic design, with ample functional spaces, including scullery, kitchen, laundry, and boiler room for the housekeeper or maid, in addition to well-proportioned living areas, bedrooms and bathroom facilities for the owners.

In a letter to Catherine Moody in November, 1977, Ronald Leigh wrote from The Orchard:

> In your letter to the *Gazette* you asked anyone living in a house designed by Troyte Griffith to get in touch with you. He designed this house for my sister in 1931. He also designed Greyroofs, higher up this road in 1907, which became my mother's a little later, where she lived until she died. It had the most delightful large terraced garden that I have known. Troyte Griffith once told me that a garden should be considered as an outdoor extension of the house and that its design was important, so I should think he was also responsible for this. Both these houses were built by W. James and Son of Upper Colwall. This combination of architect and builder surely ensured good results. When this house was being built T. G. came frequently to watch the work and make suggestions for detail. On one occasion he invited me to his house, at the Lower Wyche, to show me the many sketches he had made in Spain. He had been awarded a scholarship to study art and architecture there.

This letter confirms the observations gleaned from other sources that Troyte Griffith was clearly much involved in the details of construction of all the buildings he designed. It would be interesting to discover what became of the 'many sketches he had made in Spain' to which Ronald Leigh refers, possibly made during his tenure of the RIBA's Ardenwinkle scholarship in 1897.

The interior view of the hall and stairs illustrates a typically simple but pleasing wooden staircase, similar to that found in several other houses.

Troyte made a watercolour sketch of The Orchard which is in the possession of Chris Moir. It gives a remarkably accurate impression of how the property still looks to this day.

Chris and Terry Moir, the current owners of The Orchard, have kindly provided the following account of their impressions of living in a house designed by Troyte Griffith:

The Orchard, Peachfield Road, front aspect.

The Orchard, Peachfield Road,
view of the rear from the garden.

The Orchard, Peachfield Road,
interior view showing the hall and stairs.

Sketch of The Orchard by Troyte Griffith.

We first saw The Orchard in 1984, a rather sad, neglected stucco rendered edifice with a bright green, glazed tile roof, surrounded by tall trees, and I thought 'Art Deco Odeon Cinema,' and I disliked it intensely. We were persuaded to revisit it some three weeks later, and this time, we fell in love with it. Nothing had really changed – the faded paintwork, the drive piled high with dead leaves and the untidy garden, but somehow it just looked different, and so we bought it.

Shortly after we moved in, there was a knock on the door and a very dapper old gentleman greeted us, and said that he had seen us moving in, that he had worked for James Builders and had helped to build the house back in the 1930s, and would we like to hear about it? We spent a very pleasant afternoon hearing stories about Arthur Troyte Griffith and his periodic visits and off-plan changes over a period of several years as the house slowly took shape. We have the hand drawn, watercolour plans of the house, a work of art in themselves, and a charming concept sketch of the front elevation which shows little change to this day.

The Orchard is a true 'Gentleman's Residence' – sturdy, plain with good proportions, and a green baize door to the kitchen and scullery, with a set of (still working) servant's bells. The hall, stairs and main reception room have American oak floors, giving a warm and opulent feeling, but all of the internal windowsills were red quarry tile – a notable feature of many 1930s houses, rather austere and utilitarian, which we have now capped with matching oak sills. The brick fireplaces have the initials of the builder carved discreetly in one corner. Even the external cast iron guttering is decorated.

The back of the house faces south, overlooking just under an acre of gently sloping garden. When you stand there and look back, the house has all the appearance of a Mediterranean villa, with slatted shutters on the upper windows, roller blinds to the lower, and a sun loggia with garden doors into the two main rooms. A superb wisteria decorates the entire south facing wall, and one end of the house has a raised outside hammock room – the hooks were still there, with a clear view of the southern stretch of the Malvern Hills – a great place to waste a few summer hours.

The house is set back across the common and is then approached by a long tarmac drive down through trees to a parking and turning area big enough for five or six cars. It used to have two entrances, but the other was sold off to the house in front many years ago – the old golf club house from the time when Peachfield Common was the local golf course.

Over the last twenty-seven years we have turned the old apple orchard back into a garden, built ponds and a bandstand (we have yet to have it christened by a real band, so a CD of the Brighouse and Rastrick has had to do) and while modernising kitchen and bathrooms and maintaining decoration, we have tried to keep the house very much as it was when it first came to life. The only real structural change has been to add double glazed doors from (what is now) the dining room onto the garden.

With thick walls and a fully boarded loft, the house is warm in the winter, cool in summer, and (apart from the north facing entrance hall) light and airy throughout. We have eleven neighbours, and unfortunately we own all of the fences, but the house is quiet and private, and has superb views to the hills and over the Vale of Evesham. We are told that the green roof acts as an aiming spot for one of the holes on the nearby golf course and it stands out like a beacon when walking the hills. When snow falls and collects on the roof, beware the thaw, as it comes off in a huge avalanche all at once.

Looking back over the years, are we pleased to have owned it? A resounding 'yes,' a great family home, a charming example from a passing age and a tribute to the design skills and vision of a very unusual local architect, who built it for the son of a local family who lived half his time here and half in Spain, and whose portrait still lives in the loft. On a warm summer's evening you can still smell pipe smoke and hear the gentle clink of a glass and the creak of a hammock.

The positive feelings about their experience of living in a Troyte Griffith house, as recorded above, is in no way untypical of the reactions encountered when talking to other house owners whilst collecting material for this book. It certainly mirrors the feelings of the author and his wife about their house.

Withybrook

Further up Peachfield Road, on the corner of King Edward's Road, is the bungalow Withybrook, built in 1938. This was designed by Troyte Griffith for Mr Porter, the builder, on his retirement. Mrs Hughes, Porter's grand-daughter, wrote to Catherine Moody to tell of her family's friendship with Troyte that arose from their close working relationship on a number of building projects over the years, including All Saints Church. She also described Troyte's characteristic appearance, with his Norfolk jacket, ancient hat, German cloak and his famous bicycle, as Catherine reported in her 1978 lecture during the Malvern Fringe Festival.

The bungalow is pleasantly proportioned, now with Velux windows that were added later to allow more light into the upstairs rooms in the roof, and a good-sized garden on the corner plot.

Withybrook, King Edward's Road.

Delve End, Sexton Barns and Manningtree

A group of three houses near the corner of Albert North Road and Cockshot Road, all built to similar internal designs, was erected by Broad Builders in 1912–1914, and provides good early examples of Troyte's domestic architecture. Two of these, Sexton Barns and Manningtree, have rendered external walls, whilst Delve End is clad in Malvern Stone in a 'crazy paving' type of pattern known technically as polygonal walling. Mr A. Weston Priestley, the director of education for Worcestershire, bought Delve End from C. C. Broad, in 1920 and lived there until his death in 1947. His widow continued to occupy the house until it was sold to Major and Mrs W. Robertson-Smith in 1961, and the house was purchased by the current owners in 2007. Thus the house was occupied by only two families over a period of about eighty-seven years.

Each of these houses provides relatively spacious and comfortable accommodation, with well-proportioned rooms, but not in any way 'grand' like some of Troyte's larger houses. The generous entrance hall, central staircase, with stained glass window providing light at the top,

Delve End, Cockshot Road, rear view from the garden.

Delve End, internal view of the hall and stairs.

Manningtree, Albert Road North, rear view from the garden.

Manningtree, front aspect.

and wide upstairs corridor, all add to the sense of spaciousness. All three houses have good-sized, relatively flat gardens, although one of them, Delve End, has recently lost the charming orchard that used to run alongside the property to developers, with the creation of a large new house next door in Cockshot Road – rather too close for comfort, in the author's undoubtedly self-interested opinion.

Each of this group of houses has undergone some additions and alterations over the last hundred years or so, but they retain much of their original character and proportions. Troyte Griffith himself designed the garage ('motor shed') and small garden room extension for Delve End, so he was clearly not averse to modifying his initial plans, if required to do so.

Elsdon

Another fine house, Elsdon, was designed and built in 1922/23 for Mr and Mrs W. S. Edwardsson in Malvern Wells. Once again, the builder was W. James of Upper Colwall. The house is set back some distance from the east side of the Wells Road and approached along a curved and downward sloping drive, flanked by trees and shrubs, so that it cannot be seen from the main road. This spacious residence is splendidly situated in a commanding position with a large, terraced garden and magnificent views across open countryside, looking towards Bredon Hill. There is also a small single storey cottage adjacent to the main house, presumably built originally to house the gardener or other domestic staff.

Like several other examples of Troyte's work, perhaps the finest external aspect of the house is seen from the rear, looking back from the garden. However, as pointed out by Catherine Moody, Elsdon is handsome all round and Troyte was never one to hide things like drainpipes at the rear of the building, behind an impressive frontage.

Internally, there is a large reception hall with some fine oak panelling, an impressive stone fireplace, and a large leaded window towards the rear giving a splendid view across the valley. Other rooms are pleasingly well-proportioned, mostly with excellent views from the windows, and there is another good example of Troyte's interesting wooden staircases.

Talking about Elsdon in her 1978 lecture, Catherine Moody concluded:

This house exemplifies another element in this architect's nature. One element we have seen was that of medieval simplicity and straightforwardness, as derived from William Morris. Another is disregard for money values. His family were sufficiently affluent not to be worried about money and their interests were beyond money-making – they were intellectuals. Therefore, when Troyte Griffith tackled the job of making a shelter and a civilized home it would not enter his head to skimp on materials. No expense would be spared for the most efficient drain pipes. Walls must be solid – 'a wall is a wall' – one might paraphrase. The banishment of deep mouldings from the skirting boards, and plaster mouldings from the cornice, and the change to four-inch skirting boards and quarry tiled window sills imposes a different state of mind on the inhabitant.

Clearly, Catherine was very impressed with Elsdon and regarded it as one of the finest examples of Troyte's work.

Elsdon, Malvern Wells, front aspect, viewed from the north.

Elsdon, view from the rear of the house looking east over the Severn plain.

Elsdon, rear view from the garden.

Elsdon, panelling and fireplace
in the reception hall.

Elsdon, detail of the stairs.

Beacon's Lea

Beacon's Lea, situated in Brockhill Road, is one of the few Troyte Griffith buildings mentioned in Brooks and Pevsner's book on the buildings of Worcestershire, in the section on West Malvern. Here it is simply described as 'a pink-rendered, gabled house by A. Troyte Griffith, 1924.'

This fine house is, indeed, pink-rendered and is set in a wonderful position on the west side of the Malvern Hills. It affords magnificent views over the surrounding countryside, looking towards Wales, from all the windows at the front. Like other houses reviewed in

Beacon's Lea,
interior view of the front hall.

Beacon's Lea, Brockhill Road, Upper Colwall.

this chapter, it has well-proportioned rooms and a comfortable feel, particularly enhanced in this case by the elegant wide entrance hall which stretches across the front of the building from left to right, with the front door in the centre.

Littlecroft

Littlecroft, in Mathon Road, West Malvern, was also built in 1924. It is constructed on a steeply sloping site, so that the back garden falls away quite dramatically. The external walls are rendered and a number of alterations and additions have been made over the years, particularly to the rear of the house, although the front appears to be relatively unchanged. The front elevation is somewhat unusual in having shutters around the upstairs windows. Internally, there is another good example of the wooden staircases that typify many of Troyte's designs, in this

Littlecroft, Mathon Road, front aspect.

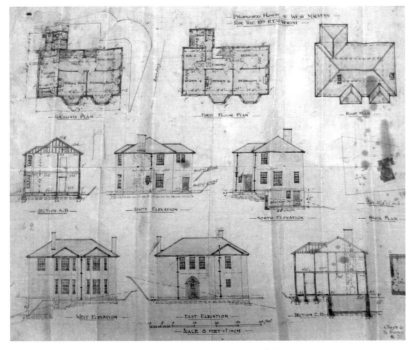

Littlecroft, original plans by Troyte Griffith.

instance painted rather than with a natural wood finish. As might be expected, the rooms are generally quite spacious and well-proportioned. There are splendid views over the surrounding countryside from the rear of the property.

This house is one of the few where the owners still have copies of the original plans, in Troyte Griffith's own fair hand.

Hay Hoe/Fox Court

The house originally called Hay Hoe, but known for many years as Fox Court, is situated down a small lane off Walwyn Road in Upper Colwall. Like several other Troyte Griffith houses, the building is well screened from the road and would be hard to find if one did not have clear directions. It was built in 1931, or thereabouts, and is another fine example of a spacious, detached house in a beautiful setting. As mentioned in an estate agent's brochure, prior to an auction sale in 1977,

Fox Court (originally named Hay Hoe), Upper Colwall, rear view from the garden.

Fox Court, view from the front drive.

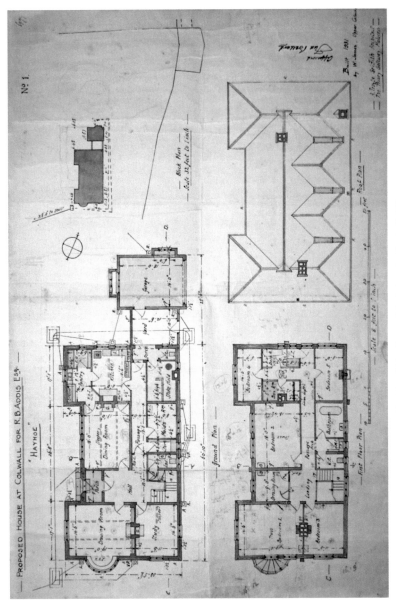

Fox Court/Hay Hoe, original plans by Troyte Griffith.

a particularly striking feature of the property is '... the delightfully proportioned rooms and the high quality of the finish throughout.'

The lovely gardens, with idyllic woodland and farmland surroundings, make this one of the best situated of all Troyte's larger houses. Internally, as one would expect, are comfortable and well-proportioned rooms, with a large stone fireplace in the drawing room and another example of the simple, but elegant wooden staircases that are so characteristic of this architect's workmanlike designs. To quote Catherine Moody again: 'An example of the Griffith style fully developed. Excellently sited and full of comfortable, solid quality.'

This is another example of a house where the owners have a copy of the original plans for the building in Troyte Griffith's hand.

Evendine Corner

There is a small group of six similar-looking semi-detached houses designed by Troyte Griffith at Evendine Corner, Colwall Green, which provide further examples of his good, functional designs for rather more modest properties than many of his other commissions. In one of these (number nineteen), there lived for many years Miss Elsie Godsell, author of several interesting booklets about Colwall. In the 1970s she related to Catherine Moody how Mr Green, a local bricklayer, first stopped outside her house and told her that the architect was Troyte Griffith. Mr Green recalled that when he was working on the construction of the house, Mr Griffith ascended a ladder to inspect the work in progress and then insisted that some eight courses of bricks had to be removed and rebuilt to his exact specifications. This seems to be a typical example of the great thoroughness and attention to details that Troyte applied to all his building projects.

Elsie Godsell, and her sister Mary, had lived for the early years of their lives on the Perrycroft Estate in Colwall, where their father was the head gardener for almost fifty years. According to Elsie Godsell, there were six cottages for staff on the estate, and the head gardener lived in one called the Lodge. The big house, Perrycroft, was designed by the famous architect of the Arts and Crafts period, C. F. A. Voysey, for the Right Honourable J. W. Wilson, MP, and built in 1893 (with later alterations and additions). According to S. Winifred

Clay Stringer, in her very detailed *History of Colwall,* a small estate of new houses was built at Colwall Green by Mr Wilson for work people, presumably to provide some affordable residences in the area. Elsie Godsell writes in her *Reflections on Colwall* that:

> Mr J. W. Wilson, late of Perrycroft, bought all the land around Blackhill and above the Brand Lodge and gave it to the Malvern Hill Conservators in order to prevent building on that part of the Hills. Mr Wilson also personally supervised the building of Evendine Corner which he built for Colwall people.

Aerial picture of houses at Evendine Corner, Colwall Green.

The land for Evendine Corner was first registered in 1913 but the houses were probably built several years later, one of them coming into the ownership of Elsie and Mary Godsell in January, 1966, from whom the current owner purchased the property in 1988.

Birkenshaw, Evendine Corner, Colwall Green.

J. W. Wilson was born in 1868 and came from one of the great Quaker families in the Midlands. He was married twice (his first wife died in 1911) and he himself died in 1932. He was said to have been 'a man of integrity, steadfastness and good judgement,' and his widow, Mrs I. Wilson also gave much of her time to public service after the loss of her husband.

Sanford
The house Sanford, in Geraldine Road, was built in 1938. It is situated in a rather more suburban and less dramatic setting than many of the other houses under consideration, on a smaller plot, but still has decent sized garden. The red brick-faced house provides comfortable family accommodation with well-proportioned rooms but no particularly note-worthy internal features to report.

Sanford, Geraldine Road.

Low Wood

Further down Brockhill Road from Beacon's Lea is another well-sited house, Low Wood. This particular house has been considerably altered over the years since it was built in 1938, with modern replacement windows and various extensions at the back. It has a splendid garden with wonderful views over the surrounding countryside.

According to Catherine Moody's notes, Troyte Griffith had vigorous arguments with the owner, Mrs Robinson, over the design of this building. One particular point of dispute concerned the windows for one of the rooms, for which she favoured a much larger size than he had originally planned. Whatever the rights and wrongs of this disagreement at the time, the original windows have long since been altered by later owners of the property.

Low Wood, Brockhill Road, Upper Colwall, rear view from the garden.

Low Wood, front aspect.

Greenwood

Situated in Jubilee Drive, near the Wyche Cutting, is one of the last known examples of Troyte Griffith's houses, Greenwood. With its elevated position, it commands fine views over the Herefordshire countryside from all the front windows. The house, built in 1939, is simple and straightforward in design, perhaps less striking than some of the larger houses, but providing characteristically spacious and well-proportioned accommodation.

Judging by photographs of the house taken in 1978, it fell into a state of some disrepair for a while. Fortunately, more recent owners have restored the building to a greatly improved and aesthetically pleasing condition.

The quality of the build clearly impressed a surveyor who carried out a survey of the property for prospective purchasers in 1984. He wrote: 'Unquestionably, this is one of the finest properties I have ever had the pleasure of surveying. In fact, in seventeen years I can think of none better.' His report concludes with the words 'If every house was designed and supervised by Mr Griffith, my work, although rewarding, would be doubly so.'

Greenwood, Jubilee Drive, Upper Colwall.

Some Architectural Features of Troyte Griffith Houses

The simple but elegant wooden staircases of several houses have been mentioned previously, and these seem to represent one recurring theme that is quite characteristic of Troyte's interior designs. Another feature seen in a few houses is the use of red bricks, or a combination of bricks and tiles, as surrounds to fireplaces, although, unfortunately, it appears that the original fireplaces have been removed and replaced in many cases. There is even one of these brick fireplaces in Troyte's own house, Fair View, which he presumably installed at some point.

A variety of different styles of fireplaces can be seen in other houses including those made of wood and stone, but it is not always easy to determine whether these are original features or later additions.

OTHER KNOWN 'TROYTE' BUILDINGS

The Wyche Institute, Malvern Wells.

The Wyche Institute

The Wyche Institute at Lower Wyche, close to All Saints Church, is the first building to be registered under Troyte Griffith's own name in the Malvern Urban District Council Register of Plans. The owners were recorded as 'the Institute Committee' and the plans were entered on 1 August, 1906. The building is set into a difficult sloping site where the gradient is approximately one in three. A new room was added to the original building in 1915.

The building currently houses the Wells 'n' Wyche Pre-school, as well as other activities such as All Saints Sunday School, Brownies, Rainbows, martial arts, camera and yoga clubs.

Abbey School (now Abbey College)

Between 1919 and 1929, Troyte Griffith was engaged by Miss Florence Judson to make a number of additions and alterations to the Abbey

Abbey School Chapel (in 1977).

Interior of Abbey School Chapel
(in 1977).

School in Malvern Wells. Notable amongst these was the chapel, illustrated here in photographs from about 1978, and the library (originally designed as a gymnasium). Perhaps inevitably over the years, the original buildings have been considerably modified and adapted to serve the needs of a modern, international school.

As mentioned previously, there are almost certainly other buildings in Malvern and the surrounding area that were designed by Troyte Griffith of which the author is currently unaware or has not been able to verify their attribution.

OTHER ARCHITECTURAL WORK

In addition to the complete buildings that Troyte designed, he was also commissioned from time to time to carry out various additions and alterations to existing buildings. These included amendments to shops, extensions or additions to private houses and other properties, and the creation of garages or 'motor sheds'. One example is the sun lounge over the front porch of the Montrose Hotel.

Sun lounge over front porch of Montrose Hotel, Graham Road, Malvern.

Plans exist of a rather grand-looking classical building for a proposed new water cure/spa development at Rose Bank Gardens which were drawn by Troyte in association with A. W. S. and K. M. B. Cross of 46 New Bond Street, London, w1 (Peter Smith, personal communication). The architects Alfred and Kenneth Cross were father and son who worked together in a practice that specialised in the design of public baths and swimming pools. Kenneth Cross became president of the RIBA in 1956–1958. Unfortunately, the drawings for the Rose Bank Gardens scheme are undated and it is not known who originally commissioned this work, but, in any case, the project never came to fruition. Since the plans are signed 'Troyte Griffith', rather than 'Nevinson and Newton', it is probable that they were prepared sometime after 1908 when Troyte started to practice in his own name from the Priory Gateway address. As mentioned in John Handley's recent book about C. W. Dyson Perrins, it is known that this prominent Malvern resident and benefactor bought Rose Bank House and Gardens in 1918 and presented them to the town, so it is tempting to speculate that he might have been behind the scheme. However, there appears to be no hard evidence to support this suggestion.

As well as practising as an architect, Troyte also did some teaching at the Malvern School of Art and gave occasional talks on architecture to local groups. One such talk, entitled the 'Architecture of Malvern', was given to the Society for Education in Citizenship and was reported in considerable detail in the *Malvern Gazette* of 25 May, 1935. A quotation from this lecture states:

> The best and most characteristic feature of Malvern is the general lay-out of the district on Garden City lines. Nowhere will you find fifty yards of closely built houses on both sides of the road. Malvern must have been at least fifty years ahead of any other town in England in avoiding the worst result of the nineteenth century commercialism – the creation of slum areas!

Headings for different parts of this talk were 'Survival of Barbarism,' 'Mediaeval Buildings left in Malvern,' 'Waters "A Cure for Cancer",'

'Favourite Resort for Honeymoon Couples,' 'Interesting Modern Structures,' 'Gothic Revival Houses,' 'Public Buildings: Library and Banks,' and 'Malvern College.' It must have been a fascinating and highly informative presentation.

Troyte Griffith also presented a paper on the 'Priory Gateway, Great Malvern' to the members of the Malvern Field Club on 28 June, 1940. This was printed in the 1940 Annual Report of the Malvern Field Club, as referred to by Pamela Hurle in her booklet about the Abbey Gateway which was published by the Malvern Museum in 1986. Quite why the gateway in question is sometimes called 'Priory Gateway' and at other times 'Abbey Gateway' is not entirely clear to the author.

A FINAL THOUGHT

Troyte Griffith was a highly competent architect, well respected in the Malvern area, who created a number of fine buildings. His houses are generally quite spacious, well-proportioned, functional and comfortable to live in, without being in any way showy or ostentatious. In addition, they are often beautifully sited in attractive situations, surrounded by generously-proportioned gardens. He was not, perhaps, in the premier league of architects of his generation, nor did his work ever achieve wide national or international recognition, but he did leave a fine legacy of excellent buildings, firmly based in the Arts and Crafts tradition.

CHAPTER THREE
TROYTE GRIFFITH:
THE ARTIST AND DESIGNER

From his early days as a child in Oxford, and later in Harrow, Troyte was inevitably exposed to the influence of artists and intellectuals of various types through his parents and their many interesting family and professional connections. Certainly he appears to have acquired a love of art and an appreciation of fine buildings during his formative years.

Watercolour paintings

Troyte Griffith was a prolific painter in watercolours but the current whereabouts of many of his fine paintings are not known. Sadly, few examples of his work are on permanent public display, although exhibitions of some of his pictures have been held in Malvern from time to time.

The first known example of his watercolours is a small sketch of Druries House at Harrow School, of which his father was housemaster.

After Troyte's death in January 1942, a Memorial Exhibition of his watercolour paintings was put on by

Druries House, Harrow School
(where George Griffith was housemaster).

his friend Victor Moody at the Malvern School of Art. The exhibition was opened by Mr A. W. Priestley, the County Director of Education, who said during his address that:

> It was hard to say whether Mr Troyte Griffith could be best described as a an architect who spent his leisure time in water-colour painting, or as a water-colour painter who spent his spare time as an architect. He mixed both interests very happily together.

Fareham Mill.

According to the report on the exhibition in the local paper, there were about eighty pictures on display, of which around twenty were of local views in the Malvern district. Other subjects that were represented included scenes from Cornish villages, Worcester, Ludlow, Rye, Bridgenorth, Durham, Tewkesbury, Canterbury, Richmond, Winchester and St David's. Most, if not all, of Troyte's output as a painter seems to have been of landscapes or of architectural subjects, human or animal figures rarely appear in his pictures.

Miss Lilian Griffith, Troyte's youngest sister, said it was a joy to know how much her brother was appreciated, and she thanked all who had had anything to do with the exhibition.

One picture that almost certainly appeared in the Memorial Exhibition was Troyte's painting of Fareham Mill. This belonged to Victor Moody, and, later, passed to his daughter Catherine.

Edward Elgar is known to have owned several of Troyte's paintings, probably including the following view of the Malvern Hills, looking south towards British Camp.

Malvern Hills, looking towards British Camp.

This picture was given by Elgar's daughter, Mrs Carice Elgar Blake, to Dr Percy Young, one of Elgar's distinguished biographers. I am extremely grateful to Mrs Renée Morris Young for kindly allowing this highly atmospheric picture to be reproduced here. It has appeared as an illustration on at least two LP record sleeves.

Another picture known to have been in Elgar's collection is currently owned by Arthur Reynolds, who lives in the USA. Mr Reynolds recently wrote to the author saying:

> Over the past half century I have assembled an archive
> of objects and documents relating to Sir Edward and his
> friends. Attached you'll find a Troyte watercolour that ranks

high among my proud possessions. The painting depicts the cathedral of Coutances painted by Troyte in March 1904 while the three-day Elgar Festival was going on in London at Covent Garden. Troyte was unable to attend the Festival because he had committed himself to be on the other side of the Channel, having accepted a bursary to paint a series of northern French cathedrals. The painting was a *mea culpa* gift from Troyte to Elgar and later hung in Elgar's bedroom at Severn House.

It would be fascinating to learn what became of the other pictures that Troyte painted in northern France during the tenure of his bursary.

An exhibition of Troyte Griffith's paintings was mounted in 1998 as part of the Autumn in Malvern Festival, organised by Peter Smith and David Prentice. In the informative booklet that accompanied this exhibition, the artist David Prentice wrote:

Watercolour of Coutances Cathedral in northern France, painted by Troyte Griffith in 1904.

The watercolours that Troyte made of the Malverns and of the medieval glass in Malvern Priory are themselves rather enigmatic. The technique he uses is simple almost to the point of being pedestrian. The landscape paintings are always purely topographical in intent. He is a very reliable narrator of what was to be seen. He never elaborates or speculates beyond the appearance of what he chooses to paint. This combination of prosaic method and simple reportage is very moving because we feel we can absolutely trust him to describe how Malvern looked in Elgar's time.

In addition to showing paintings from the private collections of several individuals, this significant exhibition showed a number of pictures that belong to the Malvern Library. These pictures are currently kept in storage under the care of the County Museum at Hartlebury, and the author has been granted permission to use digital images of some of these as illustrations, as shown on the following pages.

Malvern Priory Gateway.

The Malvern Hills, view to the south.

View near Birchwood Lodge.

View looking from Malvern out over the Severn plain.

Willows on the River Avon, Tiddington House Garden, Stratford-on-Avon.

The River Severn
near Upton-upon-Severn.

Great Malvern Priory and churchyard, view from the north-west.

Worcester Cathedral, as seen from the river.

Watercolour of glass from Great Malvern
Priory's east window.

Watercolour of glass from Great Malvern
Priory's north nave aisle.

Carved Reredos from St John
the Baptist Church, Bere Regis.

Church Interior Designs

The very fine reredos with painted panels at All Saints Church, Lower Wyche, designed by Troyte, has been mentioned previously when describing the church. He was also responsible for another reredos at the Church of St John the Baptist, Bere Regis, executed entirely in wood without any additional embellishments, such as gilding or paintwork. Troyte's brother-in-law, the Revd Montague Acland Bere, was vicar here from 1905–1919. He and Troyte's sister, Sarah L. T. Griffith, were the parents of Rennie Bere.

The *Studio* journal of 1910 includes a brief description, together with a black and white photograph, of an altar frontal designed by Troyte Griffith for St Andrew's Church in Pau, France. It is described as being:

> … embroidered in appliqué on a white figured silk, the roses and stems are chiefly in gold thread and the leaves green velvet; the doves, grey and silver; and the olive branches a beautiful French lacquered leather with silver stitching.

The superfrontal was worked by a Miss Huggett, of Brighton, and the frontal by one of her pupils, who presented it to the church.

The chaplain of the Anglican St Andrew's Church of Pau in the French Pyrenees, from 1885 to 1922, was the Revd Reginald Acland Troyte. He was also Troyte Griffith's uncle, hence the reason for Troyte's involvement with the church.

Reginald Henry Dyke Acland Troyte (1851–1932) was the eighth child (out of nine) of Arthur Henry Acland Troyte (1811–1857) and Frances Williams (Acland Troyte). He was the youngest brother of Troyte Griffith's mother, Harriet Dyke Acland Troyte (Griffith; 1838–1921). Arthur Troyte Griffith evidently visited his uncle in Pau from time to time.

Recent contact with Father Ian Naylor and the good people of St Andrew's Church led to the rediscovery of Troyte's altar frontal, still in

Altar frontal from St Andrew's Church, Pau.

good condition. They have very kindly sent a colour photograph of this splendid piece, which is illustrated above. Further information about this most interesting church can be found on the St Andrew's website at: www.standrewschurchpau.org.uk

Theatre Designs

Three years before the Pau altar frontal was completed, Troyte Griffith also became involved with designing the stage sets for a theatrical production. The play in question was *The Devil's Disciple* by George Bernard Shaw and it was put on at the Savoy theatre in London in November, 1907. It is not at all clear how Troyte became involved with this work or when he first met Shaw, and he does not appear to have undertaken any other theatrical designs before or after this particular show. However, it seems likely that the connection between the two men arose from their shared membership of the Fabian Society.

Troyte's friend Edward Elgar went to see the production in London and wrote on 4 November, 1907:

I say we went (on your account) to the Savoy on Saturday night to see *The Devil's Disciple* – it's a poor play, with moments of power: *badly* acted all round – if they had frankly gone in for melodrama it would have been fine – but they were attemptedly (that's a good word) serious and the thing lacks conviction: Shaw is very *amateurish* in many ways.

The scenery is good. Why did you date the pastor's house 1777 the year of the play? Is he just married or has he built a new house for his dreary bride, Miss Matthison: she was good in *Everyman* but only fair (she's dark, brunette, really) in this play.

The Devil's Disciple was Shaw's eighth play, written in 1897. It was first performed in London, but the American production in the same year was his first real financial success. The play has been described as 'George Bernard Shaw's biting satire on puritanism, set during the American Revolution.' The events take place in the autumn (fall) of 1777, during the Saratoga Campaign, and tells the story of Richard Dudgeon, a local outcast who is the 'Devil's Disciple' of the title. One

Hanging Scene from *The Devil's Disciple* at the Savoy theatre in 1907, sets designed by A Troyte Griffith.

Further Scenes from *The Devil's Disciple* at the Savoy theatre in 1907, sets designed by A Troyte Griffith.

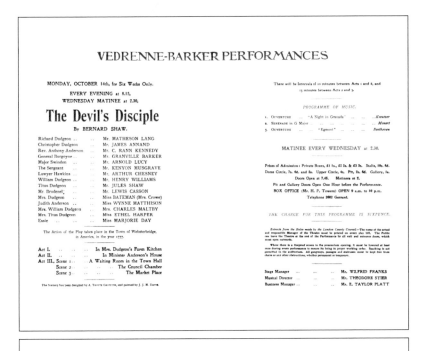

Programme for *The Devil's Disciple* at the Savoy theatre in 1907.
Detail from programme for *The Devil's Disciple* at the Savoy theatre in 1907,
showing the name of the set designer.

of the characters who appears in the play is the real-life General John Burgoyne, who eventually surrendered on behalf of the British army at the Battle of Saratoga.

Whilst attempting to find out a little more about the 1907 production, I learned that the famous Mander and Michenson Theatre Collection had recently been acquired by the University of Bristol Drama Department (Theatre Collection). With the kind assistance of the curator, Heather Romaine, a copy of the original programme and several photographs were found in the collection.

The actor/producer, Harley Granville-Barker was clearly very pleased with Troyte's contribution to the production, writing to him on 31 August, 1907 as follows:

Dear Mr Troyte Griffith,

I have just got the detailed drawings. Words fail me to express my admiration of you. I have never had so much trouble taken off my hands before. I'll write to you on Monday or Tuesday about Act III Scene 3. I think I know what is inevitable.

Yours very sincerely,
Harley Granville-Barker

In a subsequent letter, Granville-Barker explained that he was unable to accept Troyte's offer to work with him on a forthcoming production of *Arms and the Man* due to shortage of time. He expressed the hope that they would be able to co-operate again. Unfortunately, this wish does not appear to have been fulfilled.

Graphic Designs

It is thought that Troyte designed the letterhead for the Worcestershire Philharmonic Society that was used for a while by Edward Elgar. In a letter to Troyte from London, dated 16 September, 1914, he writes 'I had mentioned your assistance when we got out the simple design for the Wor. Phil. Scy.' The motto 'Wach Auf!'', which is the title of a chorus from *Die Meistersinger,* was evidently used by the Worcestershire Philharmonic, hence its inclusion on the letterhead designed by Troyte and used by Elgar.

This particular heading is shown several times in letters that are included in the book *Letters to Nimrod,* edited by Percy Young.

Troyte's own personal book plate, showing the Priory Gateway where his office was situated for many years, is quite well-known

Above left: Bere family bookplate designed and cut by Troyte Griffith for Sally.
Above right: Letterhead from Worcestershire Philharmonic Society, designed by Troyte Griffith, as used by Edward Elgar for some correspondence.

and is illustrated elsewhere in this book. He also designed and made three charming book-plates for his nephew Rennie Bere (pronounced 'Bear') and other members of his family, each depicting a bear.

Many years earlier, Troyte had designed a bookplate for his friend Edward Elgar.

Bere family bookplate designed and cut by Troyte Griffith for Rennie.

Bookplate designed for Edward Elgar by Troyte Griffith.

Bere family bookplate designed and cut by Troyte Griffith for M. A. B.

CHAPTER FOUR
TROYTE GRIFFITH
AND THE MALVERN CONCERT CLUB

Before venturing into a detailed account of Troyte's close friendship with Edward Elgar and his family, which began soon after he moved to Malvern in 1896, this brief chapter will describe some aspects of his long association with the Malvern Concert Club. Troyte was deeply involved with the Concert Club from the beginning, as has been so comprehensively and elegantly documented by Michael Messenger in his book *Elgar's Legacy: A Centennial History of the Malvern Concert Club,* and he continued this active involvement in the running of the club until the end of his life.

Edward Elgar's daughter, Carice Elgar Blake, could recall her father and Troyte Griffith talking about the founding of the Concert Club and drafting some rules whilst they were living at Craeg Lea in Malvern Wells. The discussions probably started some time in 1902, and continued in early 1903. Rosa Burley, headmistress of the Mount School where Elgar taught and Carice was a pupil, called at Craeg Lea on 16 March, 1903 to discuss the idea of founding a new music club in Malvern, and the Elgar diaries show that a similar discussion was held a week later over tea with Mr and Mrs Jebb Scott. The idea of the Concert Club was almost certainly Elgar's and its inception seems to coincide with the time when he withdrew from his position as conductor of the Worcestershire Philharmonic Society in November, 1902.

There is a letter to Edward Elgar from Adolph Brodsky, leader of the Brodsky Quartet, dated February, 1903, enclosing a copy of the

MALVERN CONCERT CLUB.

Programme of First Concert.

OCTOBER 31ST, 1903.

1. Quartet,   G minor.   *Volkmann.*
   DR. BRODSKY,
   MESSRS. SPEELMANN, RAWDON BRIGGS,
   AND CARL FUCHS.

2. Violin Solo.   Adagio (9th Concerto).
   Spohr.
   DR. ADOLF BRODSKY.

3. Quartet (Canzonetta).   - *Mendelssohn.*
   from Op. 12.

4. 'Cello Solo.   Adagio.   - *Locatelli.*
   MR. CARL FUCHS.

5. Quartet.   Opus. 59. No 1.   *Beethoven.*
   Allegro.
   Allegretto vivace.
   Molto adagio.
   Allegro (Theme Russe)

Members are informed that Tea can be obtained in the Hotel at a charge of Sixpence for each person.

Programme for first concert
on 31 October, 1903.

programme that was to be played at the very first concert over eight months later. By April of that year, Elgar had enlisted the help of a group of his more influential friends in Malvern to form an *ad hoc* committee for the embryonic Concert Club. Amongst these were Charles Grindrod (a local doctor), Sidney Jebb Scott and Troyte Griffith, and various meetings were held in September and October, before the first concert on Saturday, 31 October, 1903, at the Imperial Hotel (now Malvern St James Girls' School).

This opening concert by the Brodsky Quartet, which included music by Volkmann, Spohr, Mendelssohn, Locatelli and Beethoven, was followed by a meeting formally to establish the Malvern Concert Club. Edward Elgar explained that the club was being formed to satisfy the desire of people in Malvern to hear the best of chamber music, including instrumental and vocal recitals, but not to attempt to put on concerts of larger-scale orchestral music which would be outside its scope. The approach would be to programme ready-made concerts given by professional musicians, rather than to provide a stage for local, amateur performers.

At the inaugural meeting, Lord Beauchamp was elected as the first president, Edward Elgar as vice-president and chairman, and Frank Lloyd Oswell (a local bank manager) as treasurer, with Arthur Troyte Griffith and Sidney Jebb Scott as joint secretaries. In the event, Jebb Scott was soon to move away from Malvern in the spring of 1904, but Troyte Griffith remained as the honorary secretary for many years. At the time of the launch of the club, there were one hundred and thirty members who, according to Elgar (in a letter to Ernest Newman), included 'a mixed audience – many (most) very cultivated people who hear much music in London and abroad – not ignoramuses; then we have also those of Philistia and some school girls.' The annual subscription in the early days was one guinea.

Concerts were held in the afternoon in the large room of the Imperial Hotel, where tea could be taken after the performance. The first concert was evidently attended by the Elgars' friend Dora Penny, who sat with Elgar and Troyte and was introduced afterwards to Adolph Brodsky as 'Dorabella' of the *Enigma Variations*. Brodsky was at the time principal of the Royal College of Music in Manchester; he and his quartet were to become popular and quite regular performers at the Concert Club over the following years. There is known correspondence between Brodsky and Troyte up to 1925, from some of which it can be deduced that they shared an interest in chess as well as music. Brodsky died in 1929, at the age of seventy-eight.

Not long after the completion of the opening season of three concerts, at the end of June, 1904, the Elgar family moved from Craeg Lea in Malvern Wells to a new home, Plâs Gwyn, in Hereford, where they were to remain for the next seven years. This move occurred less than a week after the announcement of Edward's knighthood in the Birthday Honours List, so the Concert Club's illustrious chairman was now Sir Edward Elgar. In a letter dated 15 June, 1904, Sir Edward wrote to Troyte's sister saying 'we are sorry to be away from him (Troyte), not Malvern'. Although the cause of his apparent dissatisfaction with life in Malvern is not entirely clear, it may have been due partly to building work on the other side of Wells Road which interfered with the fine view from Craeg Lea. Troyte, the ever faithful and dependable friend, was involved in supervising the removal of household effects from the Malvern house.

Evidence of Elgar's continuing interest and involvement in the affairs of the Concert Club comes largely from correspondence between him and Troyte about programming for the concerts, particularly over the first three years of the club's existence, and to a lesser extent thereafter. There was some competition for attention from other concerts in the town in the early days, including the Broadwood Concerts and occasional celebrity concerts that were held in the Assembly Rooms, but the Malvern Concert Club somehow managed to survive and prosper. However, not everyone was initially convinced of the need for a concert club. In a letter dated 7 October, 1904, Troyte informed Elgar that Mrs Harriet Fitton, who was an excellent pianist in her own right, the mother of one of Edward's viola pupils, Isabel, and a friend of the Elgars, had declined the honour of joining the Malvern Concert Club committee. She expressed the view that 'There is no necessity for a "Concert Club" as Malvern cannot support two sets of classical concerts.' In the event the Concert Club proved to be more enduring than the Broadwood concerts, and Mrs Fitton did eventually join the committee a few years later. She remained on the committee until her death in January, 1924, aged eighty-nine, and her place was then taken by her daughter, Isabel ('Ysobel' of the *Enigma Variations*). One of Troyte's later commissions as an architect was to design a garage for Colonel G. Fitton (presumably Harriet and Edward Fitton's son, Guy) in 1938, for the family's house, Fairlea, in Zetland Road, Malvern.

Another of Elgar's 'Variations' who joined the Concert Club committee in the early days was Miss Winifred Norbury. She was associated with the club from the outset, and, with the exception of Troyte Griffith, became the longest serving member of the committee. Winifred died on 19 March, 1938, at the age of seventy-six, and had been involved with the Concert Club since 1903. Her diaries show that she had attended many of the concerts over those thirty five years and was a constant supporter of the club's activities. The Norbury family lived at Sherridge, the house where Elgar and Troyte were said to have sheltered during a storm whilst out walking.

Successful concerts continued to be organised for the Concert Club by Troyte Griffith and at the annual general meeting in November, 1910, which followed the twenty-seventh concert, he was presented with an illuminated address, signed by members of the club, in recognition of his untiring efforts on their behalf. It appears that the idea for this arose from discussions in the preceding weeks between Alice Elgar and Mrs Thurston Holland, who made the presentation to Troyte on behalf of Edward and Alice Elgar as they were away in London at the time.

The move of Sir Edward and Lady Alice Elgar from Hereford to Severn House in Hampstead, which happened on New Year's Day, 1912, took them even further away from Malvern, although Elgar remained as vice-president and notional chairman of the Concert Club.

The illuminated address presented to Troyte Griffith in 1910.

As recorded by Michael Messenger in his book about the club:

> Troyte Griffith was assiduous in maintaining the sort of relationship with visiting artists which brought them back to Malvern after their first appearance, as well as contacting 'new' artists and following up suggestions for future contacts. Whatever his musicality, he must by this time have been extremely knowledgeable about the abilities and availability of musicians and was quick to seize opportunities.

Troyte's skill as a concert organiser must have been severely tested in the ensuing years after the start of the First World War in August, 1914. The Concert Club committee decided to continue with the concert series as best they could during these difficult times but it was no longer possible to engage German musicians. Accordingly, there was a far greater concentration on British artists and ensembles, such as the Catterall Quartet, during this period. For a brief time, from February, 1918, for reasons unknown, Hilda Fitton took over as secretary of the Concert Club, but after her marriage in November, 1919, Troyte resumed his responsibilities and remained in post until his death in 1942. From about this time, he also took on the responsibilities of treasurer from Frank Lloyd Oswell.

At the end of the 1918–1919 season, the Concert Club ceased holding its concerts at the Imperial Hotel, after sixteen successful years and sixty concerts at that venue. The hotel had been bought by the Malvern Girls' College (now Malvern St James) in 1919 and so the club transferred its activities to the nearby Christchurch Memorial Hall, where the concerts were to be held for the next thirteen years. The first concert at this new venue, given by the Catterall Quartet and the pianist Marjorie Southam, was held on 6 November, 1919.

On 7 April, 1920, Alice Elgar died in London. She was buried in the churchyard of St Wulstan's Church at Little Malvern in a grave selected and designed by Troyte Griffith. Sir Edward was still a vice president of the Concert Club, but by this time his involvement in the affairs of the club was limited.

Concerts continued to be held at Christchurch Memorial Hall

throughout the 1920s and early 1930s, until the last event there on 2 March, 1932 – this was the one hundred and ninth concert in the series. The next venue to be used was the County Hotel and, by this point, Troyte Griffith had been organising the concerts for almost thirty years.

In 1932, the well-known actor and theatrical producer, Sir Barry Jackson, was elected to the Concert Club committee, becoming vice-president in 1935, and, eventually, president. Jackson was the prime mover in the Malvern Festival around that period, a festival which featured many of the plays of George Bernard Shaw. Both men were also friends of Sir Edward Elgar who, by this time, had relinquished London and moved back to live in Worcester.

Sir Edward Elgar, founder of the Malvern Concert Club and one of England's greatest composers, died in Worcester on 23 February, 1934, aged seventy-six. He was buried alongside his wife, Alice, at St Wulstan's Church in Little Malvern, beneath the simple headstone designed by his great friend of many years, Troyte Griffith. Somewhat strangely, his death did not seem to have been marked in any particular way, such as a special memorial concert, by the Concert Club. This may, perhaps, have been a reflection on the fact that Elgar had had little to do with the club in his later years, although he had kept in regular contact with Troyte until the end.

In 1937, Elgar's daughter, Carice Elgar Blake, was invited to join the Concert Club committee, thus ensuring a continuation of the connection with the Elgar family. Later, in 1941, she became both vice-president and vice-chairman. In 1938, the founder member, friend of Elgar, and stalwart supporter of the Concert Club for thirty-five years, Winifred Norbury, died. Shortly afterwards, of course, came the start of the Second World War (1939–1945), bringing more problems for those trying to put on a series of concerts. However, once again, the Concert Club managed, somehow, to continue producing excellent programmes of chamber music throughout the war.

Lord Beauchamp, who was the club's first president, had been living abroad for several years prior to his death in November, 1938. His place as president was taken by Sir Barry Jackson, as reported to a committee meeting on 8 January, 1941. At this same meeting, the chairman

(Dr L. A. Hamand, organist and choirmaster of Great Malvern Priory) proposed a vote of thanks to the honorary secretary. Sadly, Arthur Troyte Griffith died just ten days later. He had become secretary at the time of the inauguration of the club thirty-eight years earlier and, during his time in office, had been responsible for organising one hundred and thirty-nine concerts. His contribution was truly amazing and it is very much to his credit that the Concert Club is still thriving in 2011 after one hundred and eight seasons.

At an emergency committee meeting on 26 January, 1942, Margaret Nicholls agreed to take over as honorary secretary 'for the time being' and remained in post for the next twenty-one years. A letter was written to Troyte's sister Lilian 'expressing deep regret at the death of Mr Troyte Griffith and sincere gratitude for all he did for the club during the many years in which he was honorary secretary and treasurer.'

The one hundred and fortieth concert was given by the British String Quartet on Wednesday, 4 March, 1942, in the Malvern Public Library. During this concert, the audience stood in memory of Troyte Griffith, whilst a short Elegy by Julius Harrison, based on 'Troyte' from Elgar's *Enigma Variations,* was played by the quartet. This must have been a most moving and appropriate tribute to the man who had done so much to establish and run the Malvern Concert Club, despite the apparent handicap of not being a musician himself and the 'inconvenient' intervention of two world wars and various economic difficulties during his term of office.

MALVERN CONCERT CLUB.

Programme of the 140th Concert.

WEDNESDAY, MARCH 4TH, 1942, AT 3-0 O'CLOCK,
AT THE PUBLIC LIBRARY, MALVERN.

THE
BRITISH STRING QUARTET

JESSIE SNOW, *1st Violin.*   ERNEST TOMLINSON, *Viola.*

KENNETH SKEAPING, *2nd Violin.*   MAY MUCKLE, *Violoncello.*

ARTHUR TROYTE GRIFFITH,
Hon. Secretary and Treasurer, 1903-1942,
Died, January 17th, 1942.

The Audience is asked to stand during a short Elegy for String Quartet on "Troyte," from *Elgar's* Enigma Variations, by Julius Harrison (1942).

1. Quartet in D major, Op. 20, No. 4   -   -   *Haydn*

    Allegro di Molto.

    Un poco Adagio affetuoso.

    Allegretto alla zingarese.

    Presto Scherzando.

2. Serenade   -   -   -   -   -   *Hugo Wolf*

3. Quartet in G minor, Op. 10   -   -   -   *Debussy*

    Animé et très décidé.
    Assez vif et bien rythmé.
    Andantino doucement expressif.
    Très modéré. Très vif.

The Violin Recital by Albert Sammons is unavoidably postponed to April 1st.

Programme for the one hundred and fortieth concert,
two months after the death of Arthur Troyte Griffith.

CHAPTER FIVE
TROYTE GRIFFITH:
THE FRIEND OF EDWARD ELGAR

When Troyte Griffith came to live and work in Malvern in 1896, Edward Elgar and his wife Alice were living at Forli in Alexandra Road. It is not known exactly how they were introduced but it may well have been through the Nevinson family connection, since Troyte was working in the office of Edward Bonney Nevinson, who was the brother of Elgar's friend, the barrister and amateur 'cellist Basil George Nevinson.

In his biography of Elgar, Basil Maine wrote that:

> ... in 1896 he met A. Troyte Griffith for the first time, at a neighbour's house. They discovered that they shared a passion for long walks in the country, and it was this that led to the forming of a close and intimate companionship.

The neighbour referred to was Mary Francis Smart (1849–1932) who lived in a house called Glencairn, next door and set perpendicular to Forli. Miss Smart came originally from Wales, the daughter of the Rector of Denbigh, and she was a member of the Worcestershire Philharmonic Society. Elgar's part-song, *The Shower* (Opus 71, No. 1, 1914), is dedicated to her.

This first meeting was referred to some years later in a letter from Edward Elgar to Troyte, written from his house in Hampstead on 10 February, 1918:

> I have been laid up for so long that I seem to have lost touch
> with my oldest friends and you are now one of the oldest,
> although it seems but a little time since we first met at Miss
> Smart's and you talked of Jokai and 'Eyes like the Sea'.

At the time they met in 1896, both men were in their thirties, Elgar thirty-nine and Troyte thirty-two, and they got on very well together from the start. They remained close friends and kept in touch until Elgar's death in 1934, at the age of seventy-six, so their friendship spanned about thirty-eight years. In addition to their shared love of walking and the countryside around the Malvern Hills, Troyte and Elgar also at various times went for cycle rides together, flew kites, played Gossima (an early form of ping-pong) and billiards, and enjoyed crossword puzzles. They evidently engaged in lively discussions, with Elgar usually representing a conservative viewpoint whereas Troyte was more of a socialist, and they enjoyed a good joke, as revealed in some of their letters to one another.

There are over two hundred known letters between the Elgar family (mainly Edward) and Troyte Griffith, of which the first that is still available, from Edward Elgar to Troyte, is dated June, 1897. By this time they were addressed to 'Dear Troyte,' but presumably earlier communications would have opened more formally with 'Dear Mr Griffith,' followed later by 'Dear Griffith,' as was the style in those days. Troyte usually addressed his friend as 'Dear Elgar,' although he sometimes used the more familiar 'Dear Edward' in later years.

In addition to the many letters, another fascinating source of information about the close relationship of Troyte to the Elgar family can be found in the Elgar diaries, which have also been painstakingly transcribed by Martin Bird. Between 1897 and 1928, there are three hundred and seventy-five references to Troyte, mainly in Alice Elgar's hand (until she died in 1920). In these, very brief, entries he is variously referred to as Mr Griffiths, Mr Griffith, Mr G, Troyte Griffith, Troyte G, and Troyte, but the most frequent entries mention the 'Aged Ninepin', 'Ninepin' or, simply, '9pin'. Typical diary entries are '9pin for lunch (or tea),' but there are occasionally longer comments, such as that of 1 February, 1903: '9pin to lunch – very contradictious – A. (Alice) *had* to protest.'

From 1921 to 1939 the diaries of Carice Elgar Blake contain a further sixty-one entries which refer to the Griffith family. Mostly these relate to Troyte himself, but a few of them concern meetings with his brother Leopold Griffith.

The Elgars moved from Forli to a house on the Wells Road in 1899, remaining there until 1904. They called the house Craeg Lea, which is an anagram based either on the first letter of the names of Alice (A.), Edward (E.), Carice (C.) and Elgar, or, as has also been suggested, Alice's married name initials (C. A. E.) and Elgar. The new house was situated close to Troyte's residence at Lower Wyche and very near to the site where All Saints Church was built in 1903. Around this time, Troyte was a frequent visitor to the Elgars' home, often joining them for Sunday lunch.

In 1899 Elgar completed the orchestral work that contributed so much to his reputation as a composer, *Variations for Orchestra 'Enigma'* (Opus 36), commonly known as the *Enigma Variations*. This piece was dedicated to 'My friends pictured within' and it was first performed in St James's Hall in London on 19 June, 1899, conducted by the famous German conductor, Hans Richter. In this inspired and enduringly popular work, Elgar paints a short musical portrait of a number of his closest friends at the time, as well as his wife, Alice, and himself.

The fourteen 'Variations' are identified as follows:

Variation	Title	Dedication
Theme	Enigma	
I	C. A. E.	Caroline Alice Elgar
II	H. D. S.-P.	Hew David Steuart Powell
III	R. B. T.	Richard Baxter Townshend
IV	W. M. B.	William Meath Baker
V	R. P. A.	Richard Penrose Arnold
VI	Ysobel	Isabel Fitton
VII	Troyte	Arthur Troyte Griffith
VIII	W. N.	Winifred Norbury
IX	Nimrod	August Johannes Jaeger
X	Dorabella (Intermezzo)	Dora Penny
XI	G. R. S.	George Robertson Sinclair

XII B. G. N.   Basil George Nevinson
XIII *** (Romanza)   Lady Mary Lygon
XIV E. D. U. (Finale)   Edward William Elgar

Much has been written about the *Enigma Variations* in various biographies of Elgar, as well as in the centenary book specifically about this composition by Patrick Turner. In addition to the many detailed and scholarly books, a BBC film about the 'Variations' has been made, narrated and conducted by Sir Andrew Davies, a ballet based on the music was created by Sir Frederick Ashton for performance at Covent Garden in 1968, and a novel entitled *The Enigma Variations* by Brian Murphy, using the names of the different variations as the main characters, was published in America in 1981.

Elgar himself provided brief descriptions of each of the 'Variations'. For 'Variation' VII ('Troyte') he wrote:

> A well-known architect in Malvern. The boisterous mood is mere banter. The uncouth rhythm of the drums and lower strings was really suggested by some maladroit essays to play the pianoforte: later the strong rhythm suggests the attempts of the instructor (E. E.) to make something like order out of chaos, and the final despairing 'slam' records that the effort proven to be in vain.

Another suggestion about the origin of this somewhat 'stormy' variation is that it recalled Elgar and Troyte getting caught in a thunderstorm during one of their walks around Birchwood (Elgar's rural retreat at Storridge) on Sunday, 23 October, 1898. They ended up sheltering in the Norburys' house, Sherridge, near Leigh Sinton, on that particular occasion. Incidentally, Elgar mentioned in a postcard to Troyte, sent shortly after this event, that he had started writing the Troyte 'Variation'. Elgar had given Troyte the nickname 'the aged Ninepin' or 'the giddy Ninepin', and as Jerrold Northrop Moore has commented, the noise of the storm reminded him of bowling over ninepins. Moore also quoted an acquaintance of Troyte, Bertha Flexman, who recalled in a letter that:

Troyte Griffith could be direct to the point of abruptness and just as 'staccato' as Elgar portrayed him – in action, speech, and temperament. He could be difficult if anyone suggested a variation of his opinions or plans.

Bertha Flexman was the daughter of a local dentist, Robert Carless. Her father had been a member of the Malvern Chess Club for many years which may partly explain how she came to know about Troyte. Bertha was also a member of the Malvern Concert Club, another likely point of contact, and she later became a Liberal Councillor for Malvern Link. Her brief comment about Troyte's somewhat prickly and contentious nature is one of the few recorded insights into his personality, although we know that he was a stickler for things to be done properly when he was dealing with builders and other tradesmen.

The Troyte 'Variation' is marked 'Presto' (i.e. fast) in the score and is very short, usually lasting just under a minute in performance. It makes a striking contrast to the more gentle movements that are played before and after this brief rumbustious episode in the music. It is markedly different in character to the wonderful and moving 'Variation' ix ('Nimrod'), named after Elgar's German friend and publisher, August Jaeger, which is played on so many important public occasions.

Unlike some of Elgar's other major compositions, this piece was given a good first performance and it was generally well received, both by the public and by critics. The success of the *Enigma Variations* certainly helped to bring Elgar to more public prominence, and was produced at the start of a golden period of about twenty years during which much of his best known music was created and he achieved both national and international fame as composer of major importance.

It can also be argued that Troyte's inclusion as one of Elgar's named 'Variations' put his name on the international map rather more effectively than any of his considerable achievements as an architect and artist, recognition of which tends to be more local. Certainly, in modern times, internet searches based on the name Troyte Griffith yield many 'hits' that are almost entirely related to the *Enigma Variations* in one way or another, with little indication of any of his other possible claims to fame.

Elgar's *Enigma* 'Variation' VII (Troyte) – front page of original score.

According to Michael Kennedy, Elgar's daughter, Carice Elgar Blake, allegedly made the following remark about the characters portrayed in the 'Variations' after she had seen the ballet in about 1968, 'I knew them all and I disliked them all except Troyte.'

Troyte Griffith and Alice Elgar in the garden of Craeg Lea in 1899.

Dora Penny ('Dorabella'), writing as Mrs Richard Powell in her book *Edward Elgar: Memories of a Variation,* had several interesting recollections of Troyte. According to her, Sir Ivor Atkins called him 'that refreshing but highly argumentative Harrovian,' although she claimed never to have witnessed such arguments herself. She remembered Troyte, in the early days, sitting and grinning with amusement but hardly saying anything. From the rather shy, taciturn beginning of their acquaintanceship, Dora and Troyte evidently became good friends in later years, and when they were the only two 'Variations' left they met more frequently and had many talks. Dora was born in 1874, so she was ten years younger than Troyte. At the time when the *Enigma Variations* were first performed in 1899, she would have been twenty-five, whilst Troyte was thirty-five. Dora died in 1964, so for twenty-two years after Troyte's death she was the last remaining 'Variation'.

Dora recalled a visit to the Elgar Birthplace House with Troyte during the Worcester Three Choirs Festival of 1938. When she asked how it was possible for people to write such dull books about so brilliant and amusing a person as Elgar, he replied 'You must remember, they did not know him as we did.' These were the last words Troyte ever spoke to Dora before his death in 1942.

The correspondence between the Elgars and Troyte was often about rather mundane matters, such as coming to lunch, travelling plans, or other practical arrangements, but it also frequently reveals their shared sense of humour. Odd phrases, such as 'it would be japey to see you,' and 'mouldy japes' occur quite commonly and they clearly set out to amuse one another in some of their written exchanges. Both men seemed to have enjoyed word games and puzzles, as well as vigorous arguments and sharing jokes with one another.

For example, Troyte wrote to Elgar from Graham Lodge, Graham Road, on 4 October, 1898:

> Dear Elgar,
>
> I am glad you have at last satisfied the critics – and yourself, but remember I am one, what have you been feeding them on in London.
>
> Caractacus will be immense C'est moi qui vous le dit – French – and I ought to know as I have heard more of it than anyone else except Mrs Elgar and your cook.
>
> Which reminds me that I didn't buy Mrs Lynn Linton's cooking stove because it fetched more than the published price; such is the power of Literature. I don't think Art is quite such a draw, but what should you say to a cheap line of Elgar's Musical Cooking Stoves, Caractacus pattern, plays airs out of this celebrated composer's works while the kettle boils. Each stove tested under the special supervision of the Composer, tunes changed at frequent intervals, on a small subscription to the central foundry.
>
> Aren't you fearfully excited about Caractacus, supposing it

doesn't sound right or you have made a mistake somewhere.

We have had lovely weather here I have been lunching on the Ragged Stone on Sundays. That's better than the bar parlour of any Leeds hotel.

Please remember me to Mrs Elgar she may have forgotten me.

Yours faithfully.

A. Troyte Griffith.

History does not record whether they ever patented the suggested Musical Cooking Stove. The humorous strand in the correspondence was continued in December, 1900 with a spoof letter from 'Orlando Howle' (alias Edward Elgar) to Troyte Griffith asking him to set some (dreadful) sentimental verses to music, as Dr Elgar was too busy to set them himself.

Troyte's reply to Orlando Howle continued very much in the same vein, stating that 'It is however a fixed rule of music never to stand in the way of a brother artiste.' In a postscript to his letter, he went on to ask, 'Would you feel inclined to supply the song words for my projected sacred opera – *Jonah* – the more solid portions are already in hand by another local poet. If willing please quote lowest terms per gross of lines. No line containing less than two dozen letters to be counted.'

Writing to Troyte from Wales, Elgar addressed his letter of 12 June, 1901 to 'Dear Gruffydd,' evidently because he was learning the 'langwidge.'

Of course, not all of the letters were so light-hearted. Following the death of Troyte's father, George Griffith, Elgar wrote from Craeg Lea on 11 May, 1902, with an extra line added by Alice:

My dear Troyte:

Your letter came as a great shock to us here and we are deeply grieved – we send our sincerest condolence to you all.

I should have written at once but have had another fearful chill inside.

I trust, dear old man, all is settling down without any extra worries – the great sorrow is sufficient trial – anyhow you have our good wishes.

Yours ever,

Edward Elgar.

Very best remembrances and very sincere sympathy, we miss you so much today. [Line added by Alice].

Later that year, Elgar suggested that Troyte should consider joining the Malvern Gentlemen's Club. Incidentally, it appears that he experienced some difficulty in mastering the art of typewriting whilst composing the following typed letter:

Craeg Lea, 10 Nov, 1902.

My dear Troyte,

Although I have, much against my will, developed into a busy man since we first met, I do not cease to have the same warm feelings towards you and think over your affairs and conversations as much as ever. I have been 'smoking' a pipe over what you said about the club: naturally it is not much of an institution to attract, but it is the recognised 'respectable' haunt of the local professional men, and it has occurred to me that it might, after all, be a good thing for you to put your name up. The expense of the thing you probably have been told: I think, but am not sure, that the entrance fee is three guis. – no, the entrance is four and the annual sub. three guis. that's what I seem to remember, but Nevinson wd. say. You see, in a one-horse place like this, it means something to be in the only club, and fellows, like some of the practising architects here, wd. give one eye and half their face to be in: if you are intending to stay here, if not for ever but for a few years certain, it might be worth your while to join: don't let me persuade you, but I feel it would be right and 'elevating': you will not join in any case until the new year so we can talk it over again – if ever I am – and owed a moment's peace.

Good-bye, Yours ever,

EDWARD ELGAR.
P.S. I send this with all its 'damnèd errors' thick upon it.

Troyte did subsequently join the club and his name was included on the list of members for 1904. Many years later, a wreath was sent by members of the Malvern club for his funeral in 1942, as reported in the local paper.

Troyte also wrote occasionally to Alice Elgar. He was evidently very grateful for the opportunity to attend a rehearsal prior to the first performance of Elgar's new oratorio *The Apostles* on 14 October, 1903 in Birmingham, as revealed in the following letter, dated 9 October.

> Dear Mrs Elgar,
> The performance today was one of the greatest pleasures of my life and I must thank you properly for the privilege of being present. I am afraid I have taken these tickets rather too much as a matter of course, they come so often. I thought the scene of the betrayal one of the most affecting things in the whole range of art. It really is extraordinary that E. W. Elgar is the only modern, who can treat sacred subjects without being either absurd or disgusting, in any medium. Miss Foster was rather hard on the other singers; she ought to be condemned always to sing in that same dress. A pity she can't double the part. I am sure you will have a gigantic success on Wednesday.
> yrs sincerely,
> A. T. Griffith.

It is rather surprising that there does not seem to be any available correspondence with Troyte about Elgar's earlier choral masterpiece, *The Dream of Gerontius,* which had received its first performance three years earlier, also in Birmingham. Although this performance was not a great success for various reasons, the work was subsequently performed elsewhere to huge acclaim and later became established as one of the greatest works in the choral repertoire. However, Troyte did recall years later:

Shortly after the first performance of 'Gerontius' at Birmingham, a County Lady wrote to him: 'Lady ——— wishes to enquire what Dr Elgar's charges would be to bring his band to her garden party, and the additional charges if they remained to play dance music in the evening!' (or words to that effect).

As revealed in Kevin Allen's highly entertaining book, *Elgar the Cyclist,* Edward took up cycling in the summer of 1900. In March, 1904, he urged Troyte to follow suit in a letter written from Craeg Lea:

> It is very sad that we must go away and the thought that our plans, carried out for so many Sundays, may be disturbed is the chief factor in our grief.
>
> Now there is one very easy way for you to visit us and that is to BIKE.
>
> Now learn to ride at once and you will be able to ride on either Saturday evening or Sunday and return on Monday: your bedroom wd. always be ready and you cd. keep some old things at Plas Gwyn.
>
> I wd. not delay your experimental riding.

A little later, in July 1904, Troyte announced in a letter to Alice, written to her new address in Hereford, that he was about to learn how to ride a bicycle. At the same time he also acknowledged the recent change in title and status of the Elgars, since Edward had just been awarded his knighthood in the Birthday Honours list that was published on 24 June, 1904.

> Dear Lady Elgar,
>
> I give you all your honours! I shall be delighted to visit Plas Gwyn, next Saturday, but if you are at all in confusion, do postpone me, I have no doubt I can come any week end. I looked in at Craeg Lea on Wednesday evening. The movers seemed very careful, but their language respecting the hills of Malvern and the garden path in particular, was frequent and terse. I have got as far as a price list from Santler, a regular

Malvern one, without any prices, and shall start bicycle learning this week. Nothing except your being at the end of a bicycle ride would have brought me even as far as this! I really do or rather shall miss my visits and confabulations and I can't say how much. Love to you and Mr Elgar in many ways. I can't let you escape without some thanks.

yours sincerely,

A. Troyte Griffith.

Troyte evidently made good progress with his cycling as Alice was pleased to note in her diary on 5 November, 1904 that she went 'to meet Troyte who rode out.'

Just before the publication of the Birthday Honours List, on 19 June, Troyte had celebrated his fortieth birthday and was entertained to lunch at the Elgars' house. He also went to dinner with them on the day of the announcement of the knighthood, according to Alice's diary entry for 24 June.

Elgar evidently had a number of cycling companions with whom he liked to 'wobble around' the countryside, including several of the 'Variations' (Isabel Fitton, Winifred Norbury, Dora Penny, Troyte Griffith, George Robertson Sinclair, and Richard Baxter Townshend), as well as other friends such as Ivor Atkins (organist at Worcester Cathedral), Charles Grindrod (Malvern doctor, writer and photographer, who is famous for writing *The Shadow of the Ragged Stone,* about the legend of the hill's cursed shadow) and Rosa Burley (headmistress of the Mount School in Malvern).

The move to Hereford, together with Edward's increasingly hectic and busy life, meant that Troyte was to see less of the Elgar family than had been the case when they were neighbours in Malvern Wells. Edward's concern that their meetings had become less frequent is borne out in some of the letters, such as his letter to Troyte of 27 February, 1905, when he wrote:

It is too bad of you not to come here. I am dying of dullness! We have had three or four decent bike rides but the weather for the past week has been vile, as you know.

Later that year, on 27 December, Alice invited Troyte with the words:

> Will you come for next Sunday? Do, if you can, E. is pining to talk, he is working hard at *The Apostles,* I am thankful to say. It will be very nice if you will come and be here for N. Year's Eve. [Since part 1 of *The Apostles* was completed in 1903, it is likely that Alice was referring to part two of the work, later renamed *The Kingdom,* which was eventually completed in August, 1906.]

An important additional reason for the continuing and regular correspondence between Troyte and Elgar was the business of organising the activities of the Malvern Concert Club which Elgar had founded in 1903, as described in the previous chapter.

Elgar's great oratorio *The Apostles,* referred to previously in connection with All Saints Church, Lower Wyche, was eventually completed in August, 1903 and received its first performance at the Birmingham Festival in October of that year. This was followed three years later, not without a considerable struggle, by another oratorio, *The Kingdom,* which was first performed at the same festival on 3 October, 1906.

Troyte wrote after Elgar's death that:

> The Apostles was thought out in the porch of Queenhill Church, near Longdon Marsh. He used to ride there on his bicycle. I think he was more absorbed in *The Apostles* than in any other work written in Malvern. In fact he told me not to come until it was done.

Troyte evidently took great exception to criticism of *The Kingdom* by Ernest Newman that was published after the first performance in the *Birmingham Post,* and wrote to the editor on 5 October:

> Sir,
>
> Since the first introduction of *The Apostles* certain critics have continually reiterated that the oratorio was dull, disjointed, scrappy, and all the rest of it. Now 'E.N.' reposts in your

columns the same doleful strain over *The Kingdom*. How is it that those who crowd these uninteresting performances take such a different view from their mentors? 'E.N.' gives an answer himself. He says: 'Many people, I know, go to *The Apostles* and *The Kingdom* as they would go to church, to be morally edified. No artist can look at them from that point of view.' Now, if instead of 'artist' he were to say what he means, namely, 'critic,' the explanation is clear. Doubtless *The Kingdom* is rather trying to one who calls St Paul and St John 'vague abstractions' and 'rather colourless personages' and spends his too short time over the score in finding three hundred examples of some musical mare's nest. But for artists and amateurs, whether they are 'morally edified' or not, the composer has expressed through his music emotions profoundly felt. When this is performed with the greatest technical skill, as 'E.N.' admits, what more can be required of art?

    A. T. Griffith,
    Malvern.

He went on to write to Alice Elgar, in terms that would undoubtedly, these days, be regarded as politically incorrect:

> I hope neither you or Edward object to my letter in to-day's Birmingham Post. But I was so angry with their objectionable little Jew, I couldn't help sending some protest. I only wish it had been stronger, but as it is they have cut out one expression.
>
>   Yours sincerely,
>   A. Troyte Griffith.
>
>   P.S. I daresay I shall get down to Longdon Marsh next week. Mrs Dowdeswell has asked me to paint Eastington for her. And if it is to be done this year I must do it at once, i.e. the first fine day.
>
>   I am surprised none else tackled 'E. N.'; did you notice his parade of 'my good friend Canon Gorton'.

Incidentally, the picture of Eastington Hall, Longdon, to which

Troyte refers in the postscript, was indeed painted and is reproduced in the book *Shakespeare's Country* by John Russell, which was published in 1942.

Alice soon replied to thank Troyte for his 'Knight Errantry' on behalf of Sir Edward, in a letter written from Plâs Gwyn on 8 October, 1906.

It should perhaps be noted at this point that Edward Elgar had first met Ernest Newman in 1901 at Alfred Rodenwald's house in Liverpool, and they later became good friends, notwithstanding Troyte's obvious disapproval of some of his criticism of Elgar's work. Newman (1868–1959) wrote a book about Elgar, which was published in 1906, and became one of the most celebrated music critics of the first half of the twentieth century. In his obituary in the *Observer,* it was said of him that 'Unlike most scholars, Newman was unsurpassed as a musical journalist. The vigour of his prose and the sense of a large personality that it breathed, his wit and trenchancy as well as his learning made him beyond question the outstanding critic of his time.' Elgar dedicated his *Piano Quintet* (Opus 84) to Newman in 1919, and asked him to visit when he was on his deathbed in 1934, a meeting that Newman was to describe very movingly years later in *The Sunday Times.* Troyte himself had some correspondence with Newman between 1910–1912 in connection with the Malvern Concert Club, so perhaps he had by then recovered from his indignation over criticism of *The Kingdom.*

The humorous tone that runs through much of the correspondence between Troyte and Elgar continued on 7 July, 1908, but interspersed with a serious question about finding a suitable gravestone for Edward's parents:

> Hereford St Swithin's Day and raining 1908.
> Dear Troyte:
>   You are several kinds of Pig not to have come last Sunday. I wanted to jaw!
>   I wish you would help me over the necessary stone for my father and mother's grave: can't I have something nice? must two honest old burghers have a trade-memento – bought by the dozen? And then about material? What is possible for a

lean purse with expensive tastes? Cast off your assumed brute-selfishness and help me – I believe you wrote it out for me once but, if so it's lost and I'm knowledgeless.

Perhaps you will come over on Sunday and all will do then but something shd. be done soon.

But – are you coming?

Yours sincerely,

Ed. Elgar.

Both the children are feeling unwell: riding yesterday I asked them if we should take tea in the Village of 'Synagoguinetta'. They professed ignorance of such village; I explained it was 'Little (J.) Dewchurch'. They nearly fell off their cycles and have felt mentally incapable ever since.

Elgar later modified the name of the village for grammatical reasons, thus: 'Synagogina is open to objection as a diminutive but I have a noble thought – *Synagoghetto!*'

Elgar, like Troyte, was evidently not averse to a little Non-Politically Correct language in his writings. In the same letter, written from Hereford on 19 July, 1908, he wrote, 'Do come over: I am writing heavenly music (!) and it will do you good to hear it.'

Three years later, when Edward and Alice were contemplating a move of house from Hereford to Hampstead, the name of Troyte's former employer, Edward Nevinson, reappears momentarily. Alice wrote:

14 Feb, 1911.

Dear Troyte,

Thank you so much for sending us your friend's very nice letter. I have asked Mr Nevinson to look over the house and he says he will do so – It was good of you to send the picture, it is beautiful – I wish the nation wd. present it to Edward! – Why should they not …

Hope to see you on Thursday please keep the nice places for me and Carice. E. says he cannot come. He has nearly finished the third movement and has kept well I am thankful today –

Yrs. ever,

C. A. Elgar.

Alice wrote again later that year with some exciting news, hot off the press:

18 June, 1911

My dear Troyte,

You have shared our joys and worries for so long, you must be one of the very first to be told what I know will give you pleasure. It gives Edward the greatest pleasure, and you may suppose I am delighted and Carice. E. had a letter yesterday saying the King wished to confer the OM on him – you know that this is the one thing which really delights him, and is a splendid acknowledgement of all his work. I believe the list is to appear on Tuesday so it must not be mentioned till then, but we wanted you to know – E. is at the Hut today or wd. send love – We are invited to the Abbey for the Coronation – I do hope you are well and wish you cd. be up here. We are still hesitating about Kelston but must settle something soon.

Yrs.

C. Alice Elgar.

Troyte was clearly overjoyed to learn of his good friend's latest honour and responded immediately:

My dear Alice,

I really can't say how delighted I am to get your letter – the pleasantest surprise I have had for very many birthdays. It is kind of you to let me know – I won't let it out, but it is not lésé majesté to congratulate Edward before the announcement. 'The Hut' is rather vague as a post address, so I write to you. The OM like the VC is an honour that does mean something – it isn't 'merely a ribbon to stitch up the coat'. And I really can't think of anyone else outside who ought to be in and isn't. By rights this should have come after *The Apostles* which I still

think the masterpiece – though I believe this is heresy.
Yours sincerely,
A. Troyte Griffith.

There was also other correspondence around this time about the move to Severn House, the Elgar's grand new house in Hampstead (originally called Kelston), for which Troyte later designed some splendid bookshelves in the library.

The strong affection that had developed between Elgar and Troyte is further indicated in the letter Edward wrote on 22 November, 1911:

> Alice tells me you are thinking of buying the house, etc., etc.
> I don't know how things are purchasing property: if you want
> it I can send you say £100 and might scrape more together as a
> loan *sine die.* Tell me if I can do anything.

Troyte had rented his house for a number of years before deciding to buy it, but it is not known if he actually received any financial assistance from Edward in order to do so.

The following year Elgar reminded Troyte of a strange word that he had invented and which he had shared with his friend Sidney Colvin.

> Hampstead, 25 Sep, 1912
>
> Dear Troyte:
>
> Long ago I told Sidney Colvin of your word 'unsqueakened':
> a month or two back he had been talking to E. V. Lucas and
> E. V. L. said he shd. put it in his new book: the book is out
> – I have not seen it yet – but the Times review gives a special
> line to your word so you are, in a sort, vicariously immortal
> – E. V. L. should stand you a new pair of boots or something;
> tangible of course. I called at the Gateway but you were on
> your vagaries (possible derivation from Vaga = Hereford) For
> fear I should herein set down more matter then sense I drop
> the pen
> Yours ever
> Edwd. Elgar

It is not recorded whether Troyte ever received 'a new pair of boots or something tangible' for his efforts, but it seems unlikely.

Three years later, in 1915, Elgar was persuaded to write the music for a play entitled *The Starlight Express,* an adaptation of a novel by Algernon Blackwood, to be put on at the Kingsway Theatre in December. The designer chosen for this production was Harry Wilson, President of the Arts and Crafts Society, rather to the dismay of both Blackwood and Elgar. The result turned out to be much worse than they had feared, as Elgar explained to Troyte in no uncertain terms on 28 December, 1915:

> Your friend has entirely ruined any chance the play had of success – he's an ignorant silly crank with no knowledge of the stage at all and has overloaded the place with a lot of unsuitable rubbish and has apparently never read the play! He ought to be put in a Home!

It seems a shame that Troyte had not been invited to design the sets for this production, considering his evident success with Shaw's *The Devil's Disciple* a few years earlier.

Towards the end of 1919, Alice Elgar became very ill and on 2 April, 1920, Elgar wrote from Hampstead:

> On my return home from Leeds yesterday week I found my dear little Alice very very ill; today her heart is better but there are many attendant difficulties and she is often in great pain. All this is more of less the result of the chill in Novr – Carice and I am here always and in the deepest distress – we hope she may be better but she, poor dear, seems very much pulled down.

Sadly, the end was soon to come, as anticipated by Troyte in his reply to Edward on 7 April. Alice died on that day:

> Dear Edward,
> I am afraid from what I was able to hear from Carice on

the telephone that there is no hope for poor Alice if she has not already passed away. It is dreadful to think that I shall never see her dear face again and what it means for you and Carice I cant bear to imagine. You know what I feel so I would rather not say any more.

I went to Little Malvern this afternoon and could not get hold of the priest till eight o'clock when it was too late to write or telegraph and I did not like to telephone. Father Worswick has left and Father Campbell who has taken his place knew nothing about the grave. But I shewed him the place in the churchyard and he says you can have it if you write or telegraph to him at St Wulstan's Little Malvern. I wish I could think it would not be wanted for many years.

Yours affectly,

A. Troyte Griffith.

P.S. What was the Presbytery at Little Malvern is now a private hotel kept by a Catholic lady.

Edward received a letter of condolence from Troyte's brother, Leopold Griffith, and another from his mother, Harriet Griffith, in which she acknowledges the great importance of Alice and Edward's friendship to her eldest son.

14 April, 1920

Dear Sir Edward Elgar,

I did not like to disturb you, directly I heard of your intense sorrow, and irreparable loss – but may I now send you my deep sympathy – and gratitude. I can never forget the blessing of such a friend, as Lady Elgar has been to my son, the very best he ever had – and the happiness he has always had in your house – May it only be granted to him – that her prayers for him may be continued. Even, as we know and ... [illegible] that they are given best and unfailing support now in your greatest need.

Yrs most sincerely

Harriet D. Griffith

Troyte was much involved in procuring a burial site for Alice at St
Wulstan's Church Roman Catholic Church at Little Malvern, and in
designing the headstone. Edward was very appreciative of Troyte's help
and friendship as he expressed in a letter from his sister Pollie's house
at Stoke Prior, Bromsgrove on 19 April, 1920:

> I do not know how I shd. have got through the awfully lonely
> time without your friendship and care. As the days go by – (I
> am, with Carice, at my sister's) – the 'blank' seems greater and
> unbearable.
>
> I wish you would see if the *next space* to the little lonely
> occupied grave is to be had and if so secure it for me: I shd.
> like to know this at once and shd. be glad if you wd. have a
> simple edging of stone put round the grave or the grave and
> unoccupied space – if the latter is secured.
>
> Carice and I send our love to you.

There followed several letters on the wording for Alice's headstone,
before the details were decided.

Edward eventually sold Severn House in 1921, but continued to
live in London at 37 St James's Place until moving back to his native
Worcestershire in 1923.

He spent some of his time in London in various gentlemen's clubs,
and from one of these he wrote to Troyte with the suggestion that
he might consider becoming a member of the Savile Club in Brook
Street:

> Brooks's, St James's Street, sw1.
>
> 23 May, 1922.
>
> Dear Troyte:
>
> I wonder whether you wd. like to be member of a London
> club? I am on the committee of the Savile and if it jumped
> with your humour, wld. like to propose you: I daresay you
> know the character of the club; it is good small and not easy
> to get into. We are a good lot of fellows and everybody talks
> to everybody. I know you are not often in London but the

bedroom accommodation might be useful to you sometimes. Now I have left this till nearly the last – I have always wanted to make you a present – if you are elected (there wd. be no doubt about that) let me see you through the entrance fee and subn.!! I think it wd. be kind of you to let me do it. But after all you may jib and not want the club at all. Let me know when you are coming up and I wd. take you there on a Saturday for lunch. One other thing – if you allow me to put your name up you can withdraw it before election if you like 'without prejudice.' Sanford Terry is a member, Blackwood, etc., etc.

 Best regards,
 Yours ever,
 Edward Elgar.

Recent enquiries at the Savile Club have not yielded evidence that Troyte was ever actually proposed for membership there (Edward had been proposed by his friend Sidney Colvin, 1845–1927, who is primarily remembered for his friendship with Robert Louis Stevenson), so presumably he declined Edward's offer. Elgar resigned from the club in 1928. Earlier, in 1924, he had also resigned from the Athenaeum, to which he was elected in 1904, in protest against the election of the first Labour Prime Minister, Ramsay MacDonald, who had formed his first Government that year.

After his return to Worcestershire in 1923, Elgar sometimes used to join Troyte for his short daily excursion along the road from his office in the Priory Gateway to the Blue Bird Tea Room in Church Street, Malvern, where he enjoyed a cup of coffee and a bun. An interesting account of the Elgar, Troyte Griffith and Blue Bird Tea Room story by Peter Smith has recently been reprinted in the August, 2011 edition of the *Elgar Society News.*

Some year later, whilst living at Tiddington House, near Stratford-upon-Avon, Edward was clearly reflecting on his long friendship with Troyte when he wrote to him, somewhat wistfully, on 28 July, 1928:

Dear Troyte:
 Thank you: I thought it a pity to wait until I depart this

life and to this I want to add a word: if you want anything at any time please let me know; I must keep a certain amount invested to provide for myself (and alas! others) when the time comes when I cannot work; when I die I shall hope to leave you a little – but, to use the phrase in my former letter, I think we know each other well enough for you to ask me to 'back up' when required – without waiting for my departure from this mortal sphere. I expect you on the fourteenth and means of transport must be devised.

Yours ever,

E. E.

It is not known if Troyte ever took up this generous offer whilst Edward was alive, but he did not ultimately benefit from any specific bequest from his friend's estate. However, notwithstanding Elgar's periodic offers of help, there is no evidence to suggest that Troyte was suffering from any financial difficulties.

One of Troyte's sisters, Gertrude Griffith, met Edward in August 1933 at Marl Bank, Rainbow Hill, Worcester, his final residence. After her visit she wrote from St John's House, Taunton, where she lived with her sister Lilian, to thank him and expressed some concern about the well-being of her brother:

> Please do try and persuade my brother to have a little holiday in the nice sunny weather. Your word goes further with him than anything else!

The humour that is sprinkled throughout the long-running correspondence between Troyte and Edward Elgar, comes to the fore again in 1933 with an amusing exchange of letters between Elgar and an American piano salesman from New York, Walter Koons. This gentleman was compiling a book on *The Mystery of Music,* to which end he wrote to a number of distinguished people around the world asking for their opinions. In Elgar's reply to this request he stated:

> This I can best do in the marvellous and soul-searching words

of the philosopher, Arthur Troyte-Griffith: 'Music is the last mystery of modern life.' I would like it to remain so.

Elgar subsequently explained in a postcard to Troyte:

> As to that Yank Book – Einstein has sent its compiler a message and many others have done so. So I have said 'I will only quote the words of the philosopher, Arthur Troyte-Griffith, etc.'

The whole amusing episode has been described in much greater detail by Martin Bird in an article in the *Elgar Society Journal* (August, 2011).

Elgar's last postcard to Troyte was dictated, in Carice's handwriting, on 17 December, 1933:

> Dear Troyte,
>   I am so sorry you have a cold and hope you will soon be better although I fear the weather is not helpful.
>   Get well and come and see me as soon as you can.
>   Yours ever,
>   signed,
>   Edward Elgar.

The great friendship between Troyte and Elgar sadly came to an end when Edward died on 23 February, 1934 at the age of seventy-six. He was buried next to Alice at St Wulstan's Church, Little Malvern, in the grave selected and designed by Troyte.

Troyte's sister, Lilian, wrote a letter of condolence to Carice two months later in which she expressed concern about the effect that Elgar's death might have on her brother:

> I always feel it has been such a privilege to know your father, and to have been his 'intimate … [illegible]' – a little personally – and through his friendship with Troyte. I hate to think what a terrible blank there must be in his life now. I am hoping to come and stay with him in July – will there be any chance of seeing you then?

Left: Alice and Edward Elgar's grave in St Wulstan's churchyard, Little Malvern. Headstone designed by Troyte Griffith.

Edward and Carice Elgar, with Troyte Griffith in Malvern, c. 1902

Carice Elgar Blake's grave at St Wulstan's, Little Malvern

With love – and again deepest sympathy in which Gertrude joins.

Yrs affectly,

Lilian Griffith.

Carice Elgar Blake died in 1970, at the age of eighty, and was laid to rest at St Wulstan's in a grave next to that of her parents.

Reference has already been made to some notes that Troyte Griffith wrote about Elgar after his death. He sent these to Carice and they are now kept at the Elgar Birthplace Museum, together with the letters and diaries, and much other invaluable material relating to the life and work of Edward Elgar. In these very personal notes Troyte wrote:

> Elgar was modest about his music. I doubt if he ever used a self-laudatory expression in my hearing. When he was grousing about something he might say, 'They say I have written fine music, but I can't', etc. He liked listening to his own records and would say, 'Now listen,' or gently nudge me with his elbow. Once when we were talking about what music written since the death of Brahms was likely to last, I said, 'Well, yours and Strauss.' He said, 'Well the "Variations" may live.'

The notes continue:

> And during his last illness I put the Stratton Quartet's record of his String Quartet on the gramophone. After the slow movement I said, 'Surely that is as fine as a movement by Beethoven.' He said quite simply, 'Yes it is, and there is something in it that has never been done before.' I said, 'What is it?' He answered, 'Nothing you would understand, merely an arrangement of notes.'

Troyte was evidently rather caught out on one occasion at the Three Choirs Festival in Worcester, as he recalled below:

Elgar had a house party for a Worcester festival. On the Friday we had *The Apostles* in the morning and *Elijah* in the evening. I said to Elgar, 'I shall give *Elijah* a miss.'

'Oh, no,' said Elgar, 'you ought to go and hear it,' etc., etc. I had enough by half-time, and rather ashamed went back. I found the whole company there and was greeted with cheers. 'Here's the last of them,' said Elgar, 'how did you like *Elijah?* Why didn't you stay 'till the end?'

And Canon Gorton said: 'Well, if Elijah killed the prophets, the Apostles have killed Elijah.'

This account would appear to refer to the Worcester Festival in 1905, although the actual day when *The Apostles* and *Elijah* were both performed was Thursday, 14 September (not Friday). Alice Elgar had taken Castle House in College Green and invited several of Edward's friends, including Canon C. V. Gorton (who died in 1912). Earlier that week, on the Tuesday, Edward had received the Freedom of the City of Worcester, following which there was a performance of *The Dream of Gerontius* in the cathedral, conducted by Ivor Atkins.

Troyte was not a musician himself but, largely through his close association with Elgar, he did come to appreciate and enjoy good music. Their long companionship was largely based on a shared interest in other things, a complementary sense of humour, and simple enjoyment of one another's company. It was probably something of a relief for Elgar to be able to converse and correspond with a loyal and intelligent friend and admirer such as Troyte, and possibly helped to take his mind off other problems and pressures at difficult moments in his life, although he did conduct extensive correspondence with many other friends over the years. Their friendship was clearly an important component of Troyte's social and intellectual life, so he must have felt a great and painful loss when Edward died in Worcester in 1934, as was observed by his sister Lilian in her letter to Carice.

Without doubt, the great friendship between Troyte Griffith and Edward Elgar was beneficial and important to both of them. Had the two men never met in 1896, and had Elgar not so charmingly characterised Troyte as one of his 'Friends Pictured Within' in the

Enigma Variations, it seems unlikely that the name of Troyte Griffith would be remembered by many people these days. As it is, however, his character will be brought to life once more every time this inspired orchestral composition is played in concert halls around the world.

CHAPTER SIX
CONCLUSION

Troyte Griffith came from a distinguished and highly educated family background. During his earliest days as a child in Oxford, then later at Harrow, he would have come into regular contact with artists, scientists and other intellectuals who were friends or colleagues of his parents, and exposure to such company would undoubtedly have stimulated his interest in science and the arts. Further opportunities for intellectual development were then provided by regular contact with fellow students and teachers during his time as an undergraduate at Oriel College, Oxford, although there is little documentary evidence to reinforce this assertion, apart from a few words written many years later by a contemporary in his obituary in the *Malvern Gazette*. During the period between leaving Oxford and arriving in Malvern, Troyte spent some of his time travelling in Europe, painting, drawing and studying buildings.

Professionally, Troyte worked as an architect in Malvern from 1896 until his death in 1942, designing and creating many fine buildings in the area during his long and productive career. People who live in his houses today generally find them to be spacious, comfortable and well-proportioned, and they are often situated in highly desirable locations with wonderful views. Although he never quite achieved the national or international fame of some of his better-known contemporaries, such as C. F. A. Voysey and Sir Edwin Lutyens, he was none-the-less an accomplished and successful local architect whose work continues to be highly respected. What is, perhaps, lacking is a clearly defined and individual or trademark style that enables one immediately to differentiate his buildings from those designed by other architects.

Troyte's output as a watercolour painter was prolific and his paintings, mainly of landscapes or buildings, are much appreciated by those private collectors lucky enough to own them. It is sad that many of his publicly-owned pictures are kept in storage for most of the time rather than being on permanent public display. It would be good to establish a gallery somewhere in Malvern where a permanent exhibition could be mounted to feature the work of Troyte Griffith and other distinguished local artists, past and present. As illustrated earlier, Troyte also occasionally tried his hand at designs for the theatre and the church, as well as creating bookplates for himself and a few selected friends, which gives some indication of his great versatility as a draughtsman.

Troyte gave many years of devoted service to two local organisations, the Malvern Chess Club and the Malvern Concert Club, for both of which he acted as honorary secretary from their foundation. He was evidently a fine chess player, continuing to give fellow club members a good run for their money well into old age. Though not a gifted musician himself, Troyte rapidly became a highly effective and respected organiser of chamber concerts, clearly establishing an excellent rapport with the many artists that he was to engage on behalf of the Concert Club over the course of thirty-nine years and one hundred and thirty-nine concerts.

Without doubt, Troyte Griffith is best known outside of Malvern through his great friendship, over a period of thirty-eight years, with Edward Elgar and his family. Being one of the original subjects of the *Enigma Variations* meant that the name 'Troyte' was immortalised and, to this day, it can be heard or read in programme notes all over the world whenever this wonderful and enduringly popular composition is played. Elgar had many friends during his life, but few can have been as devoted and faithful as the ever-dependable Troyte Griffith, to whom he turned for support at various times during their long association. Country walks and cycle rides together, and frequent animated discussions about a variety of subjects over lunch or tea, must have provided great comfort and enjoyment for both men during those periods when they were living close enough to one another to indulge such pleasures. At other times, when geographically separated, they kept in regular contact by post. Troyte was equally a great favourite of Edward's wife, Alice, and also seemed to hit it off with their daughter Carice. Perhaps the contrasting political outlooks of the two men, with Elgar decidedly to the right and Troyte more to the left, coupled with the fact that Troyte was not a musician, helped to cement their close relationship through the attraction of opposites? They certainly came from rather different socio-economic backgrounds, Elgar's somewhat humbler origins and limited formal education being in stark contrast to Troyte's more privileged early life. Elgar was evidently far more of a 'Ladies Man' than Troyte, although it is impossible to know whether they ever discussed the fairer sex and affairs of the heart. A shared sense of humour, as revealed in some of their correspondence, was almost certainly another important factor in cementing their enduring friendship over the years.

Troyte was an instantly recognisable figure locally because of his tall, spare physical appearance, his slightly unusual attire, his rather strange bicycle, and his characteristic personality. He could be abrupt, argumentative and possibly, on occasions, difficult to deal with, and he was a great stickler for things to be done properly, particularly when dealing with builders and other tradesmen. He remained a bachelor all his life and no hint of any romantic attachments has been discovered whilst researching this book. All in all, Troyte Griffith was a highly talented, interesting, intelligent, versatile and industrious man, who contributed much to the local community over many years, and he was clearly a great Malvern character.

ABOUT THE AUTHOR

Jeremy Hardie is a retired microbiologist who was born and educated in London. He qualified initially as a dentist before going on to specialise in microbiology, eventually working his way through the academic ranks to become Professor of Oral Microbiology at Bart's and the London School of Medicine and Dentistry, Queen Mary, University of London. Apart from professional interests, he has always had a strong involvement in music and has sung in a number of church and chamber choirs  over the years. On retirement, he and his wife moved to the Malvern area in 2006 and now live in a house designed by Troyte Griffith. Producing this book, stimulated in the early stages by discussions with the late Catherine Moody, marks a significant (and refreshing) change in direction from the scientific research and writing in which he was previously engaged for most of his career.

Comments, corrections or suggested additions may be sent to the author at: jeremy.hardie@btinternet.com

BIBLIOGRAPHY

Allen, K., *Elgar the Cyclist,* Aldine Press (1997).

Allen, K., *Elgar in Love,* Aldine Press (2000).

Atkins, E. Wulstan, *The Elgar–Atkins Friendship*, David and Charles, (1984).

Bird, Martin 'Troyte Griffith and the Philosopher's Stone or The Hogwash Express', *Elgar Society Journal,* vol. 17, no. 2, pp.33–34, August (2011).

Brooks, Alan and Pevsner, Nikolaus, *The Buildings of Worcestershire*, Yale University Press (2007).

Burley, Rosa and Carruthers, F. C., *Edward Elgar: the Record of a Friendship*, Barrie and Jenkins (1972).

Daryl, Sidney, *Hugh Russell at Harrow: a Sketch of School Life,* Provost and Co, Covent Garden (1880). Facsimile edition reprinted in USA (2011).

De-La-Noy, Michael, *Elgar the Man*, Allen Lane (1983).

Dray, Glynis, 'A Malvern Wells Enigma: Arthur Troyte Griffith in Malvern Wells from 1896 to 1942', *Wells News,* summer (2011).

Godsell, Elsie, *Reflections on Colwall*, (1969); one of a series of pamphlets about Colwall by Elsie Godsell, kept at Colwall Library, ref. 942.447.

Griffith, Arthur Troyte, *Reminiscences of Edward Elgar*, manuscript at Elgar Birthplace Museum.

Griffith, Arthur Troyte, 'The Architecture of Malvern', report of a lecture given to the Society for Education in Citizenship, *Malvern Gazette* (25 May, 1935)

Griffith, Arthur Troyte, 'The Priory Gateway, Great Malvern', *Annual Report of the Malvern Field Club* (1940).

Griffith, Arthur Troyte, Autograph Letters Collection, Manchester Archives and Local Studies, Manchester Central Library (also available on microfilm at Malvern Library).

Handley, John L., *The Quiet Hero: the Story of C. W. Dyson Perrins 1864–1958,* Aspect Design (2010).

Harper, Wilfred, *Troyte Griffith: Architect, Artist and Enigma,* leaflet written for Malvern Tourist Information Office, two pages, undated.

Hurle, Pamela, *The Abbey Gateway, Malvern,* Malvern Museum (1986).

Kennedy, Michael, *The Life of Elgar*, Cambridge University Press (2004).

Kennedy, Michael, *Portrait of Elgar*, Oxford University Press (1968).

Maine, Basil, *Elgar: His Life and His Works*, London (1933).

Messenger, M., *Elgar's Legacy: a Centennial History of the Malvern Concert Club,* Elgar Editions (2003).

Messenger, M., *Edward Elgar,* Shire Publications (2005).

Minchin, J. G. Cotton, *Old Harrow Days,* Methuen and Co, London (1898).

Moody, Catherine, *Arthur Troyte Griffith – Memoir,* audiotape (1998).

Moody, C., *A Malvern Eccentric,* Arthur Troyte Griffith. Hand set and printed on mould-made paper at Malvern Hills College, eight page booklet, limited edition of sixty copies (1977).

Moody, C., 'Arthur Troyte Griffith 1864–1942. Enigma Variation (no. VII, "Troyte") and Malvern Character', *Elgar Society Journal,* vol. 11, no. 1, pp.2–6 (1999).

Moody, C., *The Silhouette of Malvern from Queen Victoria to Queen Elizabeth II*, the Priory Press Malvern (1953).

Moore, Jerrold Northrop, *Edward Elgar: a Creative Life,* Oxford University Press (1984).

Moore, Jerrold Northrop, *Edward Elgar: Letters of a Lifetime,* Oxford University Press (1990).

Moore, Jerrold Northrop, *Elgar: Child of Dreams,* Faber and Faber (2004).

Murphy, Brian, *The Enigma Variations: A Novel,* Blond and Briggs (1981).

Powell, R., *Edward Elgar: Memories of a Variation*, Remploy Reprint Edition (1979). First published 1937.

Reed, W. H., *Elgar as I Knew Him*, Victor Gollanz (1936).

Russell, John, *Shakespeare's Country,* Batsford (1942).

Smith, Peter, 'Elgar, Troyte Griffith and the Blue Bird Tea Room, Malvern', the *Elgar Society News,* no. 44, pp.24–25, August (2011).

Stringer, S., Winifred Clay, *History of Colwall* (reprinted 1998). First printed 1955. Colwall Library, ref. 942.42)

Sutton, Peter, *Elgar and Alice,* Sevenpix Publishing (2008).

Weaver, Cora, *A Guide to: Edward Elgar in Worcestershire,* Cora Weaver/Aldine Press, Malvern (2004).

Turner, P., *Elgar's 'Enigma' Variations,* Thames Publishing (1999).

Young, Percy M., *Alice Elgar: Enigma of a Victorian Lady,* Dennis Dobson (1978).

Young, Percy M., *Elgar OM,* Collins (1955).

Young, Percy M. (editor), *Letters of Edward Elgar and Other Writings,* Geoffrey Bles (1956).

INDEX